At Issue

The Olympics

Other Books in the At Issue Series:

At Issue

The Olympics

Tamara L. Roleff, Book Editor

GREENHAVEN PRESS
A part of Gale, Cengage Learning

GALE
CENGAGE Learning

Detroit • New York • San Francisco • New Haven, Conn • Waterville, Maine • London

Christine Nasso, *Publisher*
Elizabeth Des Chenes, *Managing Editor*

For more information, contact:
Greenhaven Press
27500 Drake Rd.
Farmington Hills, MI 48331-3535
Or you can visit our Internet site at gale.cengage.com

For product information and technology assistance, contact us at

Gale Customer Support, 1-800-877-4253

For permission to use material from this text or product, submit all requests online at www.cengage.com/permissions

Further permissions questions can be emailed to permissionrequest@cengage.com

Articles in Greenhaven Press anthologies are often edited for length to meet page requirements. In addition, original titles of these works are changed to clearly present the main thesis and to explicitly indicate the author's opinion. Every effort is made to ensure that Greenhaven Press accurately reflects the original intent of the authors. Every effort has been made to trace the owners of copyrighted material.

Cover image reproduced by permission of Gstar.

LIBRARY OF CONGRESS CATALOGING-IN-PUBLICATION DATA

The Olympics / Tamara L. Roleff, book editor.
   p. cm. -- (At issue)
Includes bibliographical references and index.
ISBN 978-0-7377-4116-2 (hardcover)
ISBN 978-0-7377-4117-9 (pbk.)
  1. Olympics. 2. Olympic Games (29th : 2008 : Beijing, China) I. Roleff, Tamara L., 1959-
  GV721.5.O3927 2009
  796.48--dc22
                                     2008028526

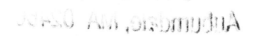

Printed in the United States of America
2 3 4 5 6   12 11 10 09 08

ED362

Contents

Introduction

The first Olympic Games were held in Olympia, Greece, in 776 BC. They were extremely popular; the stadium at Olympia could hold 40,000 spectators, and athletes from cities all over Greece competed. The Greek rulers all agreed there would be a truce before, during, and after the Games so that the athletes, their families, and spectators could travel to and participate in the Games in complete safety. The Games were held every four years until the Romans gained power in ancient Greece. The ancient Olympic Games were banned in 393 AD after Christianity became the official religion of the Roman Empire because it was said the Games were a pagan festival.

Greek philanthropist Evangelos Zappas first revived the Games in 1859, then again in 1870 and 1875. His vision for an international sports festival was taken up by Baron Pierre de Coubertin who persuaded international leaders to support the first modern Olympic Festival held in Athens in 1896.

The modern Olympics have had political troubles almost since the beginning. The 1916 Games were cancelled due to World War I, and they were cancelled again in 1940 and in 1944 because of World War II. During the 1930s, there was talk of boycotting the 1936 Games in Berlin, Germany, to protest the racist policies of Adolf Hitler. The Games did go on as scheduled, with both the Western world and Nazi Germany declaring "victory" for their side. The 1956 Summer Olympics in Melbourne, Australia, were the first Games to be boycotted. Spain, the Netherlands, and Switzerland boycotted the Games to protest the Soviet Union's invasion of Hungary. Egypt, Iraq, and Lebanon protested the Suez Crisis (in which Britain, France, and Israel invaded Egypt because it nationalized the Suez Canal) by staying home.

In 1968, two black American athletes protested the injustice faced by black Americans, by giving a Black Power salute on the winners' podium. During the 1972 Summer Games in Munich, eleven Israeli athletes were kidnapped and killed by Arab terrorists. In 1972 and 1976, many African nations threatened the International Olympic Committee with a boycott if the IOC did not ban South Africa, Rhodesia (now Zimbabwe), and New Zealand from the Games. In 1980, most Western countries boycotted the Moscow Summer Games because of the Soviet Union's invasion of Afghanistan. The Soviet Union and its bloc countries followed suit at the 1984 Olympics in Los Angeles. In 1996, an American terrorist bombed the Olympic Centennial Park in Atlanta, Georgia, killing two people and injuring 111 others.

In light of these troubles, some people maintain that the world has failed miserably in celebrating the Olympic ideals of international peace and understanding. Buzz Bissinger, an author and journalist, asserts that the "only way left to improve the Olympics [is] to permanently end them." He cites the Games' violent past and various scandals involving drugs, bribery, and corruption as reasons to end the Olympic tradition. According to Bissinger, "The loftier the rose-colored rhetoric, which in the Olympics has become an Olympian growth industry, the worse the underlying stink." All it would take to end the Olympics, he claims, is for the United States to permanently pull its athletes out of the competitions. Once the Americans have stopped competing, athletes from other countries would also stop competing, since they would no longer have world-class competition to test themselves against. And if U.S. athletes are no longer competing, it is likely that U.S. corporations would stop supporting the Games, and American television networks would stop broadcasting the Games, saving billions of dollars. Bissinger acknowledges that "some athletes [would] become innocent victims with the loss of the Olympics." But, he continues,

> It would be nothing close to the number of innocent victims killed in Darfur with Chinese-supplied weapons, or in

Iraq during the American occupation. The world would carry on without the Games. The ideals set forth by Coubertin when he revived them instead of being routinely mocked as they are now, would be honored by the admission that the Olympics have simply failed.

While Bissinger's view on ending the Olympic Games may be extreme, there are many who believe the 2008 Summer Games in Beijing should be boycotted, due to China's dismal record on human rights, its oppression in Tibet, and its support of the regime in Sudan where genocide is occurring.

Those who advocate ending the Olympic Games are in the minority, however. Most people all over the world enjoy the Games and wish for them to continue. Supporters of the Olympics contend that a boycott or cancellation of the Games would be counterproductive in that the only ones harmed by the cancellation would be the athletes. Canceling the Games would not make oppressive regimes more democratic nor would it convince the government to change its policies on human rights. George Vecsey, a sports columnist for the *New York Times*, argues that the Olympic Games have given many blessings to the world of sports. For example, he asserts that the 1996 Summer Games in Atlanta, Georgia, were great for female athletes. The American women's softball and soccer teams had real support from the U.S. Olympic Committee for the first time.

In addition, Vecsey notes that the Olympic ceremonies allow countries to honor citizens and athletes from bygone times. For example, the great American boxer "Muhammad Ali, once reviled in his homeland as a draft dodger and Muslim convert, emerged on a platform to light the Olympic flame." Furthermore, Vecsey contends, "The Olympics are always tainted." Many agree that the scandals, tragedies, and controversies that have sometimes stained the Games do not warrant the cancellation of the Olympics. These commentators believe that the Olympics have provided more benefits and good will than they have negative experiences.

The politics of the nations hosting the Olympic Games are an extremely controversial issue. The contributors to *At Issue: The Olympics* debate such timely issues as whether the games should be boycotted and the effectiveness of boycotts, commercialization of the Games, whether performance-enhancing drugs should be legalized in sport, and whether athletes who are young, transgendered, or disabled, should be allowed to compete.

1

The 2008 Olympics in China Should Be Boycotted

Sam Leith

Sam Leith is a columnist for the Telegraph, *a British newspaper.*

China has a repressive government that imprisons, tortures, and kills its political opponents. Encouraging China to improve its civil rights record by conducting business with the repressive regime does not change its policies. China can be embarrassed, however, and other countries should pressure China to change. The 2008 Beijing Olympics are a prime opportunity for the world to publicly embarrass China.

Vladimir Lenin framed the fundamental question in politics as *Kto kovo?*, or in English, "Who whom?" It is a question that frames political power in grammar. Who is nominative, and whom is accusative; who is subject and whom is object; who controls the verb and whom gets the verb in the jacksie.

It was stylishly—albeit ungrammatically—restated by Aretha Franklin in the title of her 1985 album *Who's Zoomin' Who?*

"Improvements" in Human Rights

And it has found new expression in China with the summary jailing for three and a half years of the 34-year-old human

Sam Leith, "We Should Subject China to an Olympic Boycott," *Telegraph* (UK), May 4, 2008. www.telegraph.co.uk. Reproduced by permission.

rights activist Hu Jia. Hu whom? Given that the Chinese leader shares a surname with the dissident, we could even recast Aretha: Hu's zoomin' Hu.

Good for giggles, until you read that the three-and-a-half-year jail sentence for Mr. Hu—imposed after a single day's trial—is reported to have been seen as "lenient". Had he not pleaded guilty to "inciting subversion of state power" in five online articles and two interviews with the Western media, he could have expected more.

Still, we see men in suits on the television talking about "assurances" and "improvements" in human rights that are going to be achieved thanks to the conveniently lucrative and agreeable policy of "constructive engagement".

We are encouraging China to behave in a civilised manner, they say, by doing business with them. And still, every organisation with anything like actual data on the subject seems to suggest that the Chinese state takes the money, and no notice, and goes whistling on its way.

The Olympics are ... a uniquely visible opportunity for the community of civilised nations to choose whether it gives the leadership of this revolting regime a slap on the back or a slap in the face.

To hell with constructive engagement. This is a state that imprisons, tortures and kills its political opponents. It is a state that pollutes public discourse with untruths, and that not only seeks to suppress truths, but that seeks to suppress the free exchange of thought between its citizens. It is a state that gives succour to the genocidal regime in Sudan, and has backed itself into the position of casting Buddhist monks as dangerous terrorists.

And it is a state that has so much in the way of natural resources, and manpower, and economic muscle, that it is all but immune to direct political pressure. We need them more than they need us.

When you hear [U.K. Prime Minister] Gordon Brown quack self-importantly, ahead of meetings with the Chinese premier, about how he's going to make clear in no uncertain terms that China's unacceptable stance on human rights must be improved, you think: you and Hu's army? And as Gordon comes back, boasting of his tough talking, we hear only the whine of a mosquito.

Governments Should Make a Political Stand

Yet the Chinese state is, we know, not immune to embarrassment. The energy it puts into suppressing freedoms of reporting and association are prima facie evidence of the fact that it sees information as a threat.

As [English columnist and author] Timothy Garton-Ash pointed out, it does matter a lot for Western leaders to meet and make public recognisance of the Dalai Lama: if it didn't, China wouldn't spend so much time trying to prevent it happening. And here, Gordon Brown did just the right thing.

We can go further. And, though I hear and understand the arguments that making a political stand over the Olympics unfairly penalises the athletes and politicises sport, I don't agree with them. The Olympics is already political, whatever wet-lipped witterings about the Corinthian spirit you may hear.

It is the most politics-saturated event in the whole of sport; the most political event you could conceive of. The very basis of competition is a political formation: the nation state. The decision to host it is taken by governments, the pitch funded by governments, and the boon to the host state is not economic advantage but national prestige. What's "above politics" about that?

Yes, it does seem unfair that innocent Olympians—athletes who have worked hard and for whom competing in Beijing will represent a lifetime dream—would be the ones most penalised by an boycott of some sort, while the hundreds of businesses whose trade with China directly contributes to the regime would go happily about their business.

A Prime Opportunity

But the fact is that the Olympics are—as the China government knows full well—a uniquely visible opportunity for the community of civilised nations to choose whether it gives the leadership of this revolting regime a slap on the back or a slap in the face.

So to those self-declared sophisticates who say that boycotting the Olympics would be "a futile gesture", I say: damn right. A futile gesture, visible round the world, would be just about the ticket.

And in default of an Olympic boycott it is my fervent hope that, somewhere along its London route, a brave protester—or, better yet, its bearer—takes the Olympic torch captive and extinguishes its silly flame in a puddle.

2

The 2008 Olympics in China Should Not Be Boycotted

Tim Rutten

Tim Rutten is a media critic for the Los Angeles Times.

There are two schools of thought over how to deal with totalitarian governments such as China. Some people believe that "engaging" repressive regimes will eventually lead to the state's loosening of the tight reins. Others argue that totalitarian governments must be confronted with their violations at every available opportunity. However, time has shown that neither approach changes totalitarian governments. Protests or boycotts of the Beijing Olympics will not make China leave Tibet or change its policies with Sudan.

Poetry, as Auden famously instructed us, changes nothing—and neither, despite all the predicted turmoil in San Francisco, do the Olympics.

Olympic Protests

Still, the city's entire police force and half the rest of the cops in the Bay Area, along with the Highway Patrol and the FBI, will be out, attempting to protect the Olympic torch as it makes its ceremonial passage along the Embarcadero on its way to Beijing and this summer's [2008] Games.

Thousands of protesters opposed to Chinese oppression in Tibet already have attempted to block the ceremonial run

Tim Rutten, "Olympic Protests' History of Futility," *Los Angeles Times*, April 9, 2008. www.latimes.com. Reproduced by permission.

through London and Paris. In San Francisco, pro-Tibet activists are likely to be joined by others who believe that China's close relationship with Sudan encourages Khartoum's murderous policies in Darfur.

Tibet and Darfur are particularly popular causes in Hollywood, and California Gov. Arnold Schwarzenegger endorsed the protests. (West of La Cienega [a major north-south road in Los Angeles], the Dalai Lama has higher approval ratings than Tom Hanks.) Sen. Hillary Clinton called on President Bush to boycott the opening ceremonies in Beijing. Many protesters are urging athletes to do the same; some are urging a blanket boycott not just of the opening but of the Games themselves.

Chinese conduct in Tibet and Sudan *is* reprehensible, so all this drama is cathartic in the way protests tend to be. But whether it will have much effect on China's behavior is another question altogether. If history is any guide, the answer is no.

Protests or boycotts won't get the Chinese out of Tibet or disengaged from Sudan.

The Two Camps of Olympic Protests

Essentially, the arguments over Olympic protests—of which boycotts are the most extreme—break down into two camps. One (call them the pragmatists) holds that the value of "engaging" oppressive regimes far outweighs the benefits of isolating them and that, over time, close contact with democratic societies in as many areas as possible will persuade the oppressors to change their ways. Another group (the one to which the protesters belong) argues that contact is complicity. Human rights violators, they argue, need to be forcefully confronted in every available forum.

When it comes to the Olympics, the fact of the matter is that both approaches have been tried in the past—with precisely the same negligible results. In 1936, serious movements urging an outright boycott of the Berlin Games were mounted in the United States, Britain, France, Sweden, Czechoslovakia and the Netherlands. Adolf Hitler had come to power two years after the International Olympic Committee had awarded Berlin the Games as a symbol of Germany's emergence from its post–World War I isolation.

The Olympics in Nazi Germany

By the time the opening ceremonies began, Nazi repression was in full swing, extending into areas directly involving the Olympics. In 1933, for example, all Jews were expelled from the German sports federations. In the weeks before the Games began, all the Gypsies near Berlin were confined in concentration camps. The Nazis, moreover, were quite forthright about their intention to use the Games to showcase their new "Aryan" society.

Even so, the anti-boycott forces prevailed, arguing that the best way to show the Germans their errors was to go to Berlin and compete against them. Nine Jewish athletes did win medals in Berlin, including five Hungarians and one token Jew on the German team, Helene Mayer, who had been removed from the Offenbach fencing club but ultimately was allowed to participate. There were seven Jews and 18 African Americans on the U.S. team; one was track star Jesse Owens, whose four medals made a mockery—according to the anti-boycott faction—of the Nazis' racial pretensions.

Owens' brilliance notwithstanding, the Berlin Games did nothing to alter German intentions or behavior and provided Hitler with a major propaganda victory. So much for the engagement-is-destiny argument.

The Moscow Olympics

What about the biggest boycott in Olympic history? Did that have more of an effect? The United States and 64 other countries, acting at President Carter's behest, refused to attend the 1980 Moscow Games as a protest against the Soviet Union's invasion of Afghanistan the year before. That's about as effective a protest and boycott as you're going to get. The result? The war in Afghanistan dragged on until the Soviets were forced to withdraw in 1989.

Protests or boycotts won't get the Chinese out of Tibet or disengaged from Sudan. In fact, if the Beijing regime—which has staked a lot on this Olympiad as a kind of international coming-out party—is sufficiently embarrassed, repression in Tibet may worsen because the Chinese reflexively blame that region's exiles for agitating and misleading the West.

That doesn't mean that Tibet and Darfur shouldn't be raised with Beijing whenever possible; it just means that the road to human rights in both places will—as in China itself—entail a long march rather than a quick fix.

3

Past Olympic Boycotts Have Hurt Only Athletes

Christine Brennan

Christine Brennan is a reporter for the newspaper USA Today.

The U.S. boycott of the 1980 Olympic Games in Moscow did nothing to convince Russia to leave Afghanistan. Its only effect was on the athletes who were forced to sit out the chance of a lifetime to compete against their peers from around the world. The boycott robbed an entire generation of athletes the chance to participate and compete in the world's greatest competition.

They are in their 40s now, the age when people tend to start celebrating anniversaries, if only this were one to celebrate. Why would they want to remember this? Why note the anniversary of something they were prevented from doing, the anniversary of the worst moment of their athletic lives?

The Boycott of the 1980 Summer Games

Twenty-five years ago, the U.S. Olympic Committee's House of Delegates, facing withering pressure from the Carter White House, voted by more than 2 to 1 not to participate in the 1980 Summer Olympic Games in Moscow. President Jimmy Carter ordered the boycott after Soviet forces invaded Afghanistan. Viewed through the prism of international history, you tend to forget that there were people hurt by this decision, hundreds of young athletes, torn between supporting their president in an international crisis even as they wondered how their lifetime dream had been shattered by an invasion on the other side of the world.

Some U.S. athletes sued the USOC over the decision but lost. There was nothing more they could do. The Games went on without the Americans and athletes from 64 other countries that joined the U.S.-led boycott.

"People forget what happened in 1980," said Craig Beardsley, a New Jersey kid who set the world record in the 200-meter butterfly 10 days after his Olympic race went off without him. "You meet people, and once they find out you were a swimmer, they usually ask, 'Did you go to the Olympics?' It's never an easy answer, and there's always a footnote. When they ask, 'Oh, did you get a medal?' It's kind of hard to tell them that I was not there because then you have to go into the whole story, and the last thing I'm looking for is sympathy. I just try to avoid the question and change the subject. Kind of like, 'Yeah, yeah, yeah. . . . What do you think of [U.S. Olympian] Michael Phelps?'"

Lost Opportunities

You've probably never heard of Craig Beardsley. How could you have? As he says, "1980 was one of those aberrations in time that we just happened to get stuck in." He didn't go to the Olympics, never won the gold medal that certainly could have been his, never reaped the benefits that could have been coming to a U.S. swimmer winning a big race behind the Iron Curtain. He says there is no way to know if he would have won an Olympic gold medal in Moscow on July 20, 1980, the day his race was held, but we do know that on July 30, 1980, he set the world record at the U.S. nationals, swimming a second and a half faster than Sergei Fesenko of the Soviet Union, who won the Olympic gold medal in Moscow.

Beardsley kept training, graduated from the University of Florida, waited four years for another chance at the Olympics.

Then, at 23, he missed making the 1984 Olympic team by .36 of a second. "I was devastated," he said. "I felt I owed it to so many people who had stuck with me." During the Los Angeles Games, when so much of the nation tuned in, he and his family went on vacation to Hawaii and didn't turn on the TV at all.

The Soviets didn't pull out of Afghanistan for nine years. . . . Did it put any pressure on them? No, it was just a missed opportunity for many athletes.

Years later, he would meet U.S. Olympic hockey star Mike Eruzione at a dinner in New York. "We definitely have different memories of 1980," Beardsley said with a wry laugh.

To this day, Tracy Caulkins Stockwell says when she thinks of the boycott, she feels sorriest for U.S. teammates like Beardsley, "those who didn't have another chance" in the Olympics. Caulkins, now 42 and living in Brisbane, Australia, with her husband and four children, was the USA's most dominant swimmer when she was prevented from attending the 1980 Games. She hung around for four more years and met with great success, winning three gold medals in L.A.

"What really hits home to me about the boycott was the Soviets didn't pull out of Afghanistan for nine years," Caulkins said. "Did it put any pressure on them? No, it was just a missed opportunity for many athletes. It just doesn't seem fair."

Said Beardsley, 44, who went on to work on Wall Street, "If it was going to do some good, then we could sacrifice. But as time went on, as we realized what little impact it had, I became angry for what the boycott did to all these people, my friends and teammates, and people in all those other countries too."

Returning the Favor

The Soviets and East Germans returned the favor in 1984, boycotting L.A. and lessening the competition at the 1984 Games. In a 1991 interview, Russian swimming legend Vladimir Salnikov said he still lamented not facing the Americans in Moscow in 1980, and again in L.A. in 1984. The matching boycotts robbed an entire generation of athletes on both sides of the Iron Curtain of their greatest competition on the world's grandest stage.

But time does move on, and few if any remember the anniversary anymore. "You can sit around and 'if' all day," said world champion gymnast Kurt Thomas, who would have been a favorite at the 1980 Olympics, "but eventually, you have to learn to live with it."

4

The Olympics Have Become Too Commercialized

Simon Black

Simon Black is a sportswriter for Canadian Dimension *magazine.*

The Olympics have become increasingly commercialized and now promote capitalism more than "Olympism." The International Olympic Committee acknowledges that the Games are an effective marketing tool that reach billions of people around the world. In fact, the 2008 Beijing Games are estimated to be the most profitable in Olympics history. Companies that operate in China systematically abuse China's extremely lax labor laws. The IOC should pressure the manufacturers of Olympic products to respect and follow internationally recognized labor standards.

The Olympic movement aspires to some pretty lofty goals (at least according to their website), which include "building a peaceful and better world through mutual understanding, solidarity, friendship and fair play." Such goals are embodied in the philosophy of the Olympic movement, a philosophy the International Olympics Committee (IOC) calls "Olympism." According to the Olympic Charter, Olympism "is a philosophy of life, exalting and combining in a balanced whole the qualities of body, will and mind. Blending sport with culture and education, Olympism seeks to create a way of life based on the joy of effort, the educational value of good example and respect for universal fundamental ethical principles."

Simon Black, "A Gold Medal in Hypocrisy," *Canadian Dimension*, vol. 41, September–October 2007, p. 61. Reproduced by permission of the author.

The Most Effective Corporate Marketing Platform

Compare this to the guiding philosophy of another "ism": capitalism. In its totalizing manner capitalism, too, is a philosophy of life, blending the private ownership of the means of production with (commodified) culture and (brain-numbing) education. As opposed to creating a way of life based on the joy of effort, it creates one based on the tyranny of work, the educational value of corporate "best practice" and respect for the ethical principles of, well, capitalists. As the Olympics have become increasingly commercialized and commodified—more capitalism, less Olympism—the IOC must have thought it an ideal time to hold the games in a country that spits in the face of everything the Olympic philosophy professes. And so, the 2008 summer Olympics will be held in China, a place where the Olympism creed of a "life based on the joy of effort" takes on a particularly Orwellian [referencing George Orwell's book *Nineteen Eighty-Four*, where the state maintains almost total control over its citizens] tone.

The IOC makes no bones about the commercialization of the Olympic movement; as the Committee states on its website, "the Olympic Games are the most effective international corporate marketing platform in the world, reaching billions of people in over 200 countries and territories throughout the world." By the Committee's own estimates, the Beijing Olympics stand to be the most profitable in the Games' history, set to exceed the U.S. $224-million surplus made by the Los Angeles Games of 1984. With such marketing and money-making potential, big-name athletics brands like Adidas and Nike have been in fierce competition for official Olympic Games licenses, the agreements that grant corporations the right to use the Olympic name and logo on their products. The money from these licenses is one source of funding for the Games. The Beijing 2008 website entices potential licensees with the promise of making "considerable profit through producing or selling the licensed products" and enhancing "brand image" while increasing "market share and sales."

Success at a Price

According to a new report from a global alliance of trade unions, NGOs [nongovernmental organizations] and labour groups called PlayFair 2008, the commercial success of licensees comes at the expense of their workers. PlayFair recently released the findings of their research into four companies awarded licenses to produce official Olympic goods. Their report, *No Medal for the Olympics on Labour Rights*, documents a myriad of worker-rights violations. Licensees operating in mainland China were found systematically to disregard Chinese labour laws (which are notoriously weak to begin with) in areas of health and safety, the hiring of children, wages and work hours. PlayFair notes that such transgressions are not solely the domain of Olympic licensees, but the norm in thousands of workplaces across the country (I've long thought it should be renamed the Employer's Republic of China).

PlayFair is not letting such abuses go unnoticed, and is organizing civil society to pressure the IOC to ensure the manufacturers of Olympic-branded products respect internationally recognized labour standards. With the Olympics soon headed to [Canadian] shores, we need to take up this fight now, and make Vancouver 2010 the first sweatshop-free Games.

5

Organizers Are Trying to Downplay Commercialization at the Olympics

Associated Press

The Associated Press is a U.S. news agency.

The International Olympic Committee tries hard to keep the Games free of advertising. Official sponsors are allowed to display their logos only in certain places, and the logos of companies who are not official sponsors are not permitted anywhere at any time. The rules sometimes may seem silly or bizarre, but they make the Games appear less commercialized than professional sports.

Samsung can't put its name on its popular flat-screen televisions, even in its own VIP lounge. Workers at [2006] Winter Olympic venues are taping over the Dell logos on laptops in the press boxes. The Austrians had to cover up the spiders on their Spyder jackets.

Limiting Logos and Advertising

The advertising police are out in force at the Turin [Italy] Games, enforcing arcane rules with a vigor unmatched at Olympics past.

Under International Olympic Committee rules:

- Sponsor logos are allowed, but only in certain places;

- Non-sponsors are out, no matter where;

Associated Press, "Excuse Me, But Your Label Is Showing," msn.com, February 17, 2006. Reproduced by permission.

- Venues must be kept free of advertising. Even bottles of Coca-Cola, one of the Games' biggest sponsors, have been ordered stashed out of view of the TV cameras.

"We don't want the Olympic Games becoming, let's say, a Formula 1 event where sponsors are on cars, on banners, everywhere," said Cecilia Gandini, the head of brand protection for the Turin organizing committee. Gandini can recite Olympic advertising regulations from memory and spends her days touring venues in search of violations.

"We want to protect the value of the Olympic Games," she said.

Competing Interests

The Turin clampdown underscores a tension inherent in producing the Olympics.

The games couldn't happen without huge financial commitments by corporate sponsors and broadcast partners. For the four-year Olympiad that includes the Turin Games and the 2008 Summer Games in Beijing, the IOC says sponsors and broadcasters have paid more than $4 billion—up from the $3.6 billion in such revenue the IOC collected for the 2002 Salt Lake City and 2004 Athens games.

Part of the appeal of an Olympic sponsorship . . . is the ban on venue advertising that makes the Olympics appear less commercialized than professional sports.

At the same time, the International Olympic Committee and host cities want to keep the focus on sports and avoid criticisms of overcommercialization.

"The IOC works hard to protect the investment of our partners. Without their contribution the Olympic Games couldn't happen in the way they do," said IOC spokeswoman Giselle Davies. "The balance is working extremely well."

The quest to maintain that balance leads to decisions that often seem silly. Bode Miller can't race in Sestriere with a decal for Italian pasta maker Barilla—one of his chief financial backers—on his helmet because personal sponsors aren't allowed. Nike Inc. designed patches to cover its trademark swoosh on the neck and back of the shirts for the American curling team while leaving the one on the breast. Rules permit one small trademark per garment.

Team Austria ran afoul of the IOC this week with jackets made by Spyder Active Sports that carry both the Spyder name and the company's trademark spider logo.

"They thought the spider wasn't a trademark. They covered it with tape," team spokesman Raimund Fabi said.

Sometimes the rules seem downright bizarre. At the pavilion of Samsung Electronics Co. of South Korea in a pleasant piazza set aside for exhibitions by official sponsors, flat-panel plasma TVs line the walls but don't bear the Samsung name. Neither do the laptops on display. The reason: Samsung is the IOC's official provider for mobile phones and wireless equipment. Panasonic has the TV sponsorship, while Lenovo Group Limited is supplying computers.

"That's the rules," said Sonia Kim, a Samsung spokeswoman. "We have to respect Panasonic's rights—even though we're the largest producer of plasma panels."

Part of the appeal of an Olympic sponsorship, according to sponsors and the IOC, is the ban on venue advertising that makes the Olympics appear less commercialized than professional sports.

A Vigilant Campaign

And Turin officials have been vigilant in their campaign against infringement—perhaps excessively so.

At the Palavela [an arena at the Turin Olympics], workers policed the stands of the figure- and short-track speed-skating venue to ward off "ambush marketing"—attempts by non-sponsor companies to sneak logos and brand names on TV for free advertising. The workers handed reporters swatches of black electrical tape to cover the logos of Dell Inc. laptops and told them to strip the labels off soda bottles or place them out of sight.

Davies, the IOC spokeswoman, said that sort of policing was unusual: "There may be some volunteers who have been overly enthusiastic or misunderstanding the degree to which they need to apply the policy."

Not so, said an unrepentant Gandini, the brand protection chief. "They may have been in view of the camera," she said.

One man repeatedly unfurled a banner for an online casino known for outrageous marketing stunts and Palavela workers had to ask him several times to remove it before he relented. The company declined to comment on the record about the stunt.

Sponsors believe the rules and the policing pay off. Samsung's Kim said research showed the company's brand awareness jumped 6 to 7 percent in six major countries because of its sponsorship of the Athens Olympics.

6

The Olympics Are
Too Politicized

Colman McCarthy

Colman McCarthy is founder and director of the Center for Teaching Peace and a former columnist for the Washington Post. *He teaches peace studies at four universities and three high schools in the Washington, D.C., area.*

A former Olympic athlete questions why a winning athlete's national anthem is played, and why the national flag is raised during the medals ceremony. Such nationalism and pseudopatriotism degrade the Olympics. Instead, the Olympic flag should be raised and the Olympic anthem should be played. These actions would emphasize the winners' accomplishments instead of a contest in which the athletes attempt to prove which system of government is better than another.

With much of the nation currently focused or overdosed on the [2006] Winter Olympics in Turin, Italy, few are as familiar with the spectacle—its positives and negatives—as Nathaniel Mills. An Olympian in the 1990s, he competed as one of the world's elite athletes, a long-track 400-meter speedskater who made three U.S. teams: Albertville, France, 1992; Lillehammer, Norway, 1994; Nagano, Japan, 1998. Few athletes qualify even once for the Olympics, let alone three times.

Now 34, Mr. Mills is a Chicago native who studied at Northwestern University and then earned a law degree from

Georgetown University in 2001. As one of his professors there, I came to know and admire him greatly.

Unlike some athletes who are one-dimensional, Mr. Mills sees sports contextually as an expression of a society's ethics, politics, economics and identity. He valued the games for their international flavor, their bringing together people shaped by discipline, sacrifice and confidence. He had used all of those assets himself to become a world-class skater, to the point of taking off whole semesters from college to drive himself to improve. He took six years to get his degree from Northwestern.

Nationalism and Pseudopatriotism

It was only after he retired from competition that Mr. Mills saw how nationalism and pseudopatriotism degraded the Olympics. Why, he wondered, are national flags raised at the medal ceremonies? Why are national anthems played?

If the Games become contests between hired gladiators of various nations with the idea of building national prestige or proving that one system of government or other is better than another, they will have lost all purpose.

"The simplest way to de-nationalize the medal ceremony," Mr. Mills believes, "is to raise the Olympic flag and sound an Olympic anthem when awarding the winner. The Olympic flag, representing the continents on which humanity resides and not the nation-states artificially created upon them, has become one of the most recognized positive symbols on the planet. A denationalized ceremony would simply recognize the accomplishment of the winner—and all competitors—as a victory for humankind, giving everyone cause to say, 'That is one of our own.'"

A Lost Purpose

At the 2002 winter games in Salt Lake City, where he spoke as a representative of the U.S. Athletic Commission, Mr. Mills expressed those views. He was rebuked as a dreamer, an agitator and an unpatriotic nag. His critics had forgotten what Avery Brundage, the only American ever to serve as president of the International Olympic Committee, once said: "If the Games become contests between hired gladiators of various nations with the idea of building national prestige or proving that one system of government or other is better than another, they will have lost all purpose."

Such thinking is beyond the executives of NBC, the Olympic broadcaster providing coverage—if past performance means anything—gushingly pro-American. NBC might as well become the Nationalistic Broadcasting Company. It's a high moment when an NBC camera catches a close-up of an American gold medalist's face as tears trickle down the cheeks during "The Star-Spangled Banner."

Well aware that his agitations for reform aren't likely to be enacted anytime soon, Nathaniel Mills has lately been reforming his own life. Instead of practicing law, where $100,000 salaries are common the first year out of law school, he resigned from the District of Columbia bar and began volunteering as a public high school teacher. He is a war tax refuser. As an opponent of prisons, he declines to serve on juries. He gets around Washington on a trusty bicycle and travels internationally not on a U.S. passport but on one from the World Service Authority [a nonprofit organization that supports world government].

On Saturday mornings, he's up before dawn to give skating lessons to minority children at a rink in one of the poorest parts of Washington. It's a sports story of the rarest kind, a world-class athlete who is now the class of the neighborhood.

7

The Olympics Always Have Been Politicized

Dave Zirin

Dave Zirin writes sports commentary for several newspapers, magazines, and his own Web site, www.edgeofsports.com.

The Chinese crackdown on dissenters in advance of the 2008 Olympics in Beijing is nothing new. Repressive crackdowns prior to the Olympics have been practiced for decades, and by democratic governments. While the Olympics may be the world's biggest sports showcase, it is also a prime opportunity to protest a country's politics.

There is something bizarre yet familiar about the fact that China's crackdown in Tibet has provoked more discussions on the fate of the Beijing Summer Olympics than on Tibet itself. The Games are supposed to be China's coming-out party as a 21st century economic superpower. The brutality of the clampdown on the Tibetan protesters puts this at risk.

Countries seeking a piece of China's economy have rushed to de-link the crackdown in Tibet with the Olympics. The White House headed off any talk that President [George W.] Bush would cancel his appearance at the Olympic Games when spokeswoman Dana Perino said Bush believed that the Olympics "should be about the athletes and not necessarily about politics." Earlier, the European Union said an Olympics "boycott would not be the appropriate way to address the work for respect of human rights, which means the ethnic and religious rights of the Tibetans."

Dave Zirin, "The Iron Fists before Gold Medals," *Los Angeles Times*, March 23, 2008. www.latimes.com. Reproduced by permission of the author.

A Time-honored "Tradition"

What Bush and the EU apparently don't realize is that the crackdown is not happening in spite of the Beijing Olympics but because of the Beijing Olympics. In acting so brazenly in Tibet, China reminds us that pre-Olympic repression is as time-honored as the lighting of the Olympic torch. Consider:

- In 1984, Los Angeles Police Chief Daryl F. Gates oversaw the jailing of thousands of the city's gang members, known and suspected, in the infamous "Olympic gang sweeps."

- The 1996 Atlanta Games were supposed to reveal the face of what President Clinton called "the New South." But the new version ended up looking a lot like the old one when city officials razed public housing where many African Americans lived to make way for Olympic facilities and ordered mass arrests to clear the streets of what they considered riff-raff. As Wendy Pedersen, a low-income housing organizer in Vancouver, Canada, site of the 2010 Winter Olympics, said, Atlanta passed six ordinances that "made all kinds of things illegal, including lying down" on city streets. Lots of the people were put in a jail that the Olympic planning committee built, the first project completed on schedule, according to Pedersen.

- Repression followed the Olympic Rings to Greece in 2004. As *Democracy Now*, a daily, independent news show that airs on public radio stations across the U.S., reported at the time, authorities in Athens "round[ed] up homeless people, drug addicts and the mentally ill, requiring that psychiatric hospitals lock them up." The pre-Olympics "cleanup" included detaining or deporting refugees and asylum-seekers. Being the first Olympics after 9/11, police surveillance of immigrant Muslims and makeshift mosques in Athens greatly increased.

Mexico City

- The most brutal example of Olympics-related repression came in Mexico City in 1968. The capital city had been the scene of months of university students striking and protesting for greater rights for themselves and workers. As the date of the Games approached, the Mexican government increasingly took a hard line. On Oct. 2, 10 days before the opening of the Summer Olympics, Mexican security forces fired on thousands of student demonstrators and workers gathered in the Plaza de las Tres Culturas, killing hundreds of them. Kate Doyle, director of the Mexico Documentation Project, an organization seeking to shed light on the lethal crackdown, wrote in the group's 2006 report that "when the shooting stopped, hundreds of people lay dead or wounded, as army and police forces seized surviving protesters and dragged them away."

As shocking as the Tlatelolco massacre, as it came to be known, was the coverup. "Eyewitnesses to the killings," reported Doyle, "pointed to the [Mexican] president's 'security' forces, who entered the plaza bristling with weapons and backed by armored vehicles. But the government pointed back, claiming that extremists and communist agitators had initiated the violence." Mexican authorities also spoke of "making their country secure" for the Games.

A Pre-emptive Strike

China's aim in Tibet in 2008 may be the same as Mexico's in 1968—a preemptive strike to ensure that the Beijing Games do not become a platform for protesting the Chinese government.

The irony then was that although the Mexican government succeeded in crushing any sign of protest outside the Olympic venues, it couldn't stop American Olympic athletes Tommie Smith and John Carlos from raising their black-gloved fists to protest racism and the muzzling of dissent, de-fining the 1968 Games as a stage for discontent rather than athletic excellence.

It's a lesson that the Chinese may want to consider now.

8

The Olympics Should Not Be Politicized

Ross Terrill

Ross Terrill, a research associate at Harvard's Fairbank Center, is the author of The New Chinese Empire.

China is using the Olympics as another tool to control its citizens and remake the truth. The country is banishing undesirables from Beijing and clamping down on "troublemakers" during the Olympics to give the appearance of a peaceful and harmonious society. The Chinese government hopes to use a successful and well-run Olympics as propaganda for years to come. Boycotting or disrupting the Olympics will not change Chinese policy on human rights or repression. Nor does a successful Olympics guarantee the future of Chinese Communist rule.

In China, language has long been a test of political orthodoxy. In Mao Zedong's era, to confuse evil "bourgeois" with virtuous "proletarian" was to face a prison cell. Write the Chinese character for a leader's name at a wrong angle and you were a class enemy. Now, as Beijing begins the final year of its preparations for the 2008 Olympic Games, a mistake with an English word is taboo.

Attempting to Fix Shaky English

Some lapses are harmless. "Don't Bother" as a privacy request on a hotel door, for example, or "Chop the Strange Fish" on a

Ross Terrill, "In Beijing, Orwell goes to the Olympics," *New York Times*, August 22, 2007. www.nytimes.com. Copyright © 2007 by The New York Times Company. Reprinted with permission.

restaurant menu. Others could lead to minor trouble. "Please take advantage of the chambermaids," says a resort brochure.

The penalty for "Chinglish" is usually humiliation, not incarceration. Still, citizens are asked to snitch, Mao-era style, on people who shame China with their shaky English. An outfit called the Beijing Speaks Foreign Languages Program issues prefabricated foreign phrases to workers who cannot converse in any foreign tongue. The Olympics have become one more tool in the authoritarian state's box of tricks.

Yes, curbing Chinglish—along with current efforts to eliminate spitting, littering and pushing to enter a bus or train—shows the better side of authoritarianism. Clean streets are agreeable, and Beijing's may now be better than New York's. The city's Spiritual Civilization Office has begun a monthly "Learn to Queue Day," surely welcome to all who have been victims of the scramble to board a Chinese bus. It reminds one that China could have a government far worse than it has now.

Remaking the Truth

Yet behind the attack on Chinglish lies an Orwellian [referencing George Orwell's book *Ninety Eighty-Four* where the state maintains almost total control over its citizens] impulse to remake the truth. Banished from Beijing for the Olympics will be not only fractured English, but disabled people, Falun Gong practitioners, dark-skinned villagers newly arrived in the city, AIDS activists and other "troublemakers" who smudge the canvas of socialist harmony.

Politicizing the Olympics in any fashion is shortsighted.

This summer, around the time of the 18th anniversary of the Tiananmen Square protests [1989 protests that were broken up by the military and resulted in injuries and death] the government honed house arrest as a device to smoothly eliminate dissidents. Hu Jia and Zeng Jinyan, a young couple who often speak up for rights granted in China's Constitution, and who were already veterans of hundreds of days of house arrest, were again locked up just minutes before they were to fly to Europe to show their documentary film *Prisoner of Freedom City*, which depicts the gap between fact and fiction in the political life of Beijing.

Fictions will abound for the month of August 2008. On all fronts the party-state will pull the rabbit of harmony from the hat of cacophony—"What do you mean by dissidents?" Scientists have been told to produce a quota of "blue days" with a clear sky, perpetuating a Chinese Communist tradition of defying natural as well as human barriers to its self-appointed destiny. Mao vowed to plant rice in the dry north of China as well as the lush south, to prove the power of socialism. "We shall make the sun and moon change places," he cried. None of this occurred.

Likewise, in 2001, arguing before the world to get the Olympic Games, the vice president of Beijing's bid committee said, "By allowing Beijing to host the Games, you will help the development of human rights." Yet the opposite danger looms: Games preparation has spurred repression.

Every day, government censors send news organizations a list of forbidden topics and guidelines for covering acceptable ones. The price for ignoring the list: dismissal of an editor or closure of the publication. Last spring, government supervisors even instructed the TV producers or *Happy Boys Voice*, a Chinese version of *American Idol*, to eliminate "weirdness, vulgarity and low taste." No wonder Dai Qing, a journalist who was imprisoned after Tiananmen in 1989, says the only thing she believes in China's press is the weather report.

Truth and Power

Truth and power are both headquartered in the Communist party-state. "Truth" (socialism sparkles, people adore the party) is not only enforced by the party-state but created by it. Stamp out Chinglish; ban "unhealthy thinking"; just keep the picture pretty—or else.

Sport should be just sport.

Some Americans overlook Beijing's manipulations because our culture and politics go their separate ways. The upheavals of the 1960s pulled American culture to the left, yet Richard Nixon took the White House in 1968. Today, university faculties are on the left in many states where Republicans dominate politics. Americans display an invigorating inconsistency that is beyond the imagination of the Chinese, both Communists and dissidents.

Alas, few Americans visiting Beijing next August [2008] will realize that the drinking water from the faucets of their five-star hotels is unavailable to 99 percent of the city's residents. In fact, this city's water is not safe to drink; the water for the athletes and tourists will be piped in from neighboring Hebei Province.

The Games Are Important to China

[The 2008] Olympics are far more important for China than the Los Angeles Games of 1984 were for the United States or Sydney's 2000 Games were for Australia. A regime may be at stake. With Marxism largely evaporated and Leninism fraying at the edges, the Chinese Communist Party's fate hinges on 10 percent annual economic growth and visions of national glory.

For years, the party hopes, it will be able to flaunt photographs of Tibetan farmers cheering at a Chinese gold medal in table tennis, videos of Muslims in Xinjiang Province fainting with joy as the women's high jump goes to China by half an inch over Japan, and documentaries in which Beijing taxi drivers speak in perfect English to tourists from New York.

The Games will likely be well run and successful, and that should not disappoint Westerners. Politicizing the Olympics in any fashion is shortsighted. Boycotting Beijing's 2008 show over Darfur [the Chinese government's support for the Sudanese government] would not usher in a humane Chinese foreign policy toward Africa. Disrupting it because of China's Orwellian fictions would not free the political prisoners.

The Chinese state, for better and for worse, knows exactly what it's doing, in Africa and at home. Still, a brilliant Olympic Games will be no more of a clue to the future of Chinese Communist rule than the spectacular 1936 Berlin Games were a sign of Nazism's longevity. Correct language, like a gold medal, is desirable in itself. But neither guarantees glory for a state that pursues them for political ends (ask the Soviet Union). Sport should just be sport. The democracies should insist on that and leave political manipulation to the dictatorships.

9

The Selection of China to Host the Olympics May Lead to Change

Mary-Anne Toy

Mary-Anne Toy is a reporter for The Age, *an Australian newspaper.*

China is leaving nothing to chance when it hosts the 2008 Summer Olympic Games in Beijing. It has built a new airport, launched a new weather satellite, taught children about Olympic history and principles, and made plans to eliminate pollution. The Chinese government sees the Olympics as a legitimization of its Communist rule. Despite its best efforts to control its population, the Olympics will change China and the Chinese forever. The next generation of Chinese will be the ones most likely to benefit from China's gradual liberalization.

With less than 200 days to go until the [2008 Summer] Olympics, China is preparing to dazzle the world with the most glittering spectacle ever seen.

This is the biggest "coming out" party of all. Now Beijing anxiously waits to see if its giant sporting gamble will reap the geo-political laurels it seeks.

China Transformed

Fifteen years after its failure to win the 2000 Games, which went to Sydney largely because of concerns over China's human rights record, the planet's most populous nation has

Mary-Anne Toy, "China's Gold Medal Gamble," *The Age*, February 27, 2008. Reproduced by permission.

transformed itself, overtaking Britain to become the world's fourth largest economy after the US, Japan and Germany.

China has embarked upon a buying spree to secure energy and resources on every continent, including Australia, unrivalled in scope since the US became the world's dominant power.

Beijing has used a missile to shoot down an old weather satellite to signal the start of a renewed space program that will launch its third manned space mission later this year.

It has also steadily ratcheted up its international diplomacy, to reflect its new economic power and to ensure a smooth path ahead for continued growth.

From launching a new satellite in space, to better monitor Olympic weather, to the estimated $40 billion to rebuild Beijing's transport, water and power systems and cut pollution, to educating 400 million school children about Olympic history and principles, to mobilising more than 21,000 torchbearers to carry the Olympic flame on the longest relay route in history, including scaling the top of Mount Everest, China is leaving nothing to chance.

Since the Spielberg controversy China's envoy to Darfur has renewed efforts to broker peace there.

Staggering Numbers

The figures are mind-boggling. China has spent more than $2 billion building 12 venues, including architectural icons such as the Bird's Nest national stadium and the Australian-designed Water Cube aquatic centre, plus renovating and expanding 11 existing venues and eight temporary venues.

China's new airport terminal is open for take-off. Designed to resemble a dragon, the Norman Foster–designed building will, naturally, be the biggest airport building in the world.

Another $12 billion has been poured into greening the dusty city, including 900 hectares of plants in the Olympic Green alone.

It is well on its way to replacing its 60,000 taxis and 19,000 buses with more energy-efficient models.

Most public signs have been made bilingual (with "Chinglish" gems such as the Dongda Anus Hospital renamed, in this case as the Dongda Proctology Hospital) and organisers say up to 100,000 bilingual volunteers are being recruited to help the expected 2.5 million Chinese visitors and the 550,000 foreign tourists who will descend on the capital this summer [2008] navigate around a city where English, while rapidly growing, is still far from common.

China's Goals

But will this mammoth drive be enough to convince the world that a new China will truly emerge from the Olympics, or will air pollution and food safety concerns, persistent charges of human rights abuses on everything from Tibet, religious freedom, corruption and, of course, international controversy over China's global diplomacy, particularly the situation in Darfur, Sudan, mar the nation's efforts to "enhance (positive) domestic and global publicity" and "showcase China's image as an open, democratic, civillised and harmonious country"?

The latter are two of Beijing's nine self-proclaimed Olympics goals for 2008.

The Gulf Between Western and Chinese Views

The controversy over US director Steven Spielberg quitting the Beijing Games because of alleged Chinese inaction to stop the atrocities in Sudan's Darfur region highlighted the gulf between the expectations of the Western world and domestic critics of how China should liberalise for the Olympics and how China sees its obligations—and the public relations risks inherent in "coming out" under the glare of world scrutiny.

Spielberg's decision was front-page news in the rest of the world, seen as a black eye for Beijing, but here in China it was initially ignored by the mainland press. The exception was the jingoistic *Global Times*, which said Chinese people were "disgusted" with the decision.

"Western exploitation of the Olympics to pressure China immediately provoked much disgust among ordinary Chinese people," the paper said.

"The vast majority of Chinese people have expressed bafflement and outrage at the Western pressure. In their view, it's absolutely absurd to place the Darfur issue, so many thousands of miles away, on the head of China."

Truth is, due to China's still very effective censorship, the vast majority of Chinese people didn't hear about the Spielberg story for several days, until the lumbering state-controlled media was given permission to write about the issue and attack Spielberg.

China has protested that Spielberg's linking of Darfur to the Games is against the Olympic spirit because it mixes sport and politics, but, of course, every host country uses the Olympics for political purposes.

More at Stake for China

The 2008 Beijing Games are undeniably intended to inspire awe around the world. But for China's leaders, who are steering through uncharted waters as they try to create the first successful hybrid of a capitalist, one-party autocracy, there is still more at stake: the Olympics are seen by them as a legitimisation of the Communist Party of China—a patriotic rallying point to unite its 1.3 billion, increasingly expectant citizens in times of explosive economic growth and social and cultural upheaval.

Xiao Qiang, a Chinese human rights activist and journalism lecturer now based in California, supported China's first

Olympics bid four years after the Tiananmen Square massacre [where protestors were killed by Chinese military], believing it would force reform.

He told the *San Francisco Chronicle* that dream was now lost: "It's all to a certain degree to justify the Communist Party. The Olympics is a perfect vehicle to support the official narrative."

The rest of the world should accept that China was not going to adopt Western style, multi-party democracy any time soon, but the country should be given credit for its gradual liberalisation.

Yet, since the Spielberg controversy China's envoy to Darfur has renewed efforts to broker peace there. And while it has also sought to intercede with the military junta in Burma during [2007's] monks' rebellion and with the North Korean communist dictatorship of Kim Jong-il, distancing itself from repression at home may prove more difficult.

Changing Tack for the 2008 Games

After losing the bid for the 2000 Games in 1993, China reluctantly changed tack in its campaign for the 2008 Olympic Games and pledged that the Olympics would improve human rights in China.

Now, with less than six months to go before the Games, a slew of detentions have cast doubt on that claim.

Last week [February 2008], the trial began of a land rights activist, Yang Chunlin, accused of staining China's international image because he has opposed the Olympics.

Yang, a 52-year-old retrenched factory worker, is charged with "inciting subversion of state power" after he helped gather 10,000 signatures on a petition demanding "human rights, not the Olympics."

Yang, who has pleaded not guilty, has questioned why China is spending billions on the Olympics when millions of Chinese cannot afford food and school fees.

Meanwhile, another court sentenced democracy activist Lu Gensong to four years' jail for subversion.

China Cracks Down

Others, such as blind activist Chen Guangcheng who exposed local authorities illegally forcing women to have abortions to comply with one-child quotas, are in jail, awaiting trial or have disappeared, either in hiding or in secret detention.

And [in February 2008], Shanghai human rights lawyer Zheng Enchong was repeatedly beaten by police outside his home, according to his wife and associates who said he was pivotal in organisation opposition to a new maglev (magnetic levitation) train that would have sliced through middle-class suburbs. He was seriously injured.

Heightening fears of a crackdown, formal charges of subversion were laid last month against Hu Jia, one of China's most prolific dissidents who has campaigned for AIDS patients, democratic reform and environmental protection.

Hu Jia's wife, Zeng Jinyan, a human rights activist in her own right and prominent blogger, has been imprisoned with their three-month-old daughter in their Beijing flat, with phone, internet and mobile lines cut off, since Hu's arrest on December 27 [2007].

The family's flat is in Bobo Freedom City, a typical Beijing compound of dozens of high-rise buildings next door to a massive new Olympic park, chosen as one of 26 sites across Beijing to have giant television screens for public viewing of the Games.

Some Early Releases

Balanced against the plight of Hu and others has been the early release of several prominent journalists in the past month.

They include Yu Huafeng, editor of the crusading *Southern Metropolitan News*, who was released after serving four years of an original 12-year sentence for embezzlement and graft.

Yu, and two other editors also since released, were arrested in 2004 after the newspaper reported the beating death of a man in detention and broke the news of a case of severe acute respiratory syndrome while Beijing was still denying it had any SARS cases.

Hong Kong journalist Ching Cheong was also released this month after serving three years of a five-year sentence for allegedly leaking state secrets and spying for Taiwan.

The Olympics will change this country forever despite the government wrapping it up in propaganda.

In his first public comment since his release, the 58-year-old chief China correspondent for Singapore's *The Straits Times* maintained his innocence as he called on the mainland authorities to grant amnesty to more prisoners, to enhance social harmony in the run-up to the Games.

Dissident writer Liu Xiaobo said he expected the Government would release many activists in an amnesty before the Games. Other dissidents are not so confident.

Requests for an interview with officials of the Beijing Organising Committee of the Olympic Games [BOCOG] on how China sees its obligations before the Olympics and how they are going to deal with dissent have not been answered. Despite BOCOG arranging weekly press conferences and briefings, getting answers is another matter.

The Games Are for the Chinese

A source close to Beijing's Olympic organisers said what the Western media did not get was that the Chinese see the Olympics as primarily for the 1.3 billion Chinese—despite their rhetoric about the games being for the world. "Remember that no one does propaganda better than China ... and as long as the domestic audiences are kept happy then they don't give a shit about what the foreign media write."

A boycott or any big-scale human rights campaign against China will be counterproductive.

The Olympic insider, who spoke only on condition of anonymity, says the rest of the world should accept that China was not going to adopt Western style, multi-party democracy any time soon, but the country should be given credit for its gradual liberalisation. He cites as a graphic example the history of the Workers Stadium.

Built in 1959 as Beijing's first soccer stadium, it was the Bird's Nest [China's current national stadium] of its day. During the 1960s Cultural Revolution, the sportsground was filled with thousands of Red Guards hailing Chairman Mao and cheering as class traitors were shot in the head. Come August [2008] the renovated 70,000-seater will be filled with cheering spectators with soft drinks and popcorn and the only blood spilt will be from the Olympic boxing matches it will host.

Change Will Come

"The Olympics will change this country forever despite the government wrapping it up in propaganda—governments come and go," the Olympic insider said. "There will be a wave of patriotism, nationalism that will negate any foreign protests.

"Chinese people are excited about the games, they can see this as a way of joining the international community and even though the gulf in understanding will remain between the West and China, the bigger story that isn't being written is that some 400 million schoolchildren in China are now reading IOC-approved materials teaching them about universal values such as fair and honest play. It's the next generation, the post-Olympics generation where you will see change."

Political observer and author Sidney Rittenberg, who lived and worked in China for 35 years after World War II, including 16 years jail when Mao Zedong suspected him of being an American spy, says a boycott or any big-scale human rights campaign against China will be counterproductive.

"These Games aren't the property of the Communist Party—they are a national event in the heart of virtually every Chinese and anything perceived as an attack on the Games is going to make ordinary Chinese people angry and resentful and that's not what we want," Rittenberg said.

"This is the first time in 5000 years of history ... that China has really joined the world and increasingly so it is moving towards what (former US deputy secretary of state) Robert Zoellick called a 'responsible stakeholder.'"

10

The Choice of Beijing as Host Will Not Open Up the Country to Democracy

Arch Puddington

Arch Puddington is director of research for Freedom House, an organization that promotes freedom and democracy around the world.

In designating China as the host country for the 2008 Summer Olympic Games, the International Olympic Committee is repeating its errors of choosing fascist Germany in 1936 and Communist Russia in 1980. It is absurd to think that sport—including the Olympics—is independent of politics. Berlin and Moscow used the Olympics in their propaganda war against the West, and Beijing is sure to follow suit. The IOC is more interested in having China clean up the smog-ridden air for the athletes than in having China improve its repressive policies and deplorable human rights abuses against its own citizens. There is no evidence that having the Olympics in Beijing will make any difference in the suffering of the Chinese people.

The "Genocide Olympics" is what Mia Farrow has called the games scheduled to open next summer [2008] in Beijing. The actress has been protesting China's role in facilitating the slaughter in Darfur, but her efforts have not exactly generated a groundswell of support (unless one counts a single

Arch Puddington, "China Games," *Commentary*, vol. 124, no. 4, November 2007, pp. 55–59. Copyright © 2007 by the American Jewish Committee. All rights reserved. Reprinted from *Commentary*, November 2007, by permission of the publisher and the author. All rights reserved.

tough letter to the Chinese leaders from the director Steven Spielberg, who was perhaps making amends for the embarrassment of having previously agreed to help choreograph the opening ceremonies of the games). Thus far, despite some cosmetic gestures, Chinese policy toward the brutal regime in Sudan remains fundamentally unchanged, and the 2008 Olympics remain on track.

Nor is the Sudanese nightmare the most pressing issue arising out of the prospective games. Why, one might ask, was the People's Republic of China awarded sponsorship of the world's premier sporting competition in the first place? After all, it is not the only modern dictatorship to have been so honored—two earlier instances were Nazi Germany in 1936 and the Soviet Union in 1980—and one might think that history had provided plenty of warning signs to anyone who cared about the condition of free athletic competition. One would be wrong.

Hitler's Olympics

The 1936 Berlin games are chiefly remembered as "Hitler's Olympics." To be sure, Hitler had inherited them; the International Olympic Committee (IOC) had designated Berlin as the host city some years before the Nazi accession in 1933. But the German dictator was quick to recognize the value of this opportunity to showcase the ideal of Aryan superiority and the glories of the Nazi state. Becoming intimately involved in the preparations, Hitler made decisions on details ranging from ceremonial pageantry to stadium architecture to the appropriate display of Nazi uniforms and insignia.

He also made decisions concerning the tricky issue of the Olympics and the "Jewish problem." Almost from their first day in power, the Nazis had begun issuing decrees designed to reduce the [status] of Jews from citizens to subjects, and thence to victims. German-Jewish athletes, even the most talented among them, were not exempt from oppression.

This posed a dilemma for the IOC. While some of its leaders were made uneasy by Nazi conduct, the organization's consistent position was that a host country's political system was a matter of no concern: the Olympic movement stood above politics. Thus, neither the general climate of militarism and thuggery in Germany nor the restrictive measures placed on Jews and on Jewish athletes ever led the IOC to consider a change of venue.

Still, the right of athletes to compete regardless of race, religion, or creed lay at the heart of the Olympic ideal, and the committee could not simply ignore the issue of whether Jews would be allowed to participate on the German team. Questioned on this matter by the IOC, the Nazis invariably replied that any German citizen who met the qualifying standards would be permitted to take part. This was a lie, if one that IOC officials were happy to swallow. One of the German dictatorship's first actions had been to bar Jews from membership in sport clubs and the use of training facilities, effectively denying them an opportunity to enter the tryouts.

A Call for a Boycott

To the willful naivete of some in the IOC most be added the rank anti-Semitism of others. "There are not a dozen Jews in the world of Olympic caliber" was the succinct formulation of one official, evidently basing himself on the canard that Jews were not an athletic people. Such instinctive antipathy was exacerbated within the IOC by the growing call for an American boycott of the Berlin Olympics.

Proponents of a boycott ranged across the religious and political spectrum. But to Avery Brundage, a leading American sports official who would eventually come to sense as IOC president, the boycott was an alien and un-American idea, part of a malevolent scheme to politicize the Olympics. "[C]ertain Jews," he warned, "had better understand that they cannot use these games as weapons in their boycott against the

Nazis." As criticism of the IOC mounted, it sought a way to defuse the pressure by concocting what might be called the "one Jew" solution.

In a personal meeting with Hitler, Charles Sherrill, an American IOC representative, urged the addition of a single token Jew to the German team. Hitler adopted a variant of this proposal: Gretel Bergman, a world-class high-jumper, was invited to return home from exile in England to compete for a position. For as long as the boycott remained a threat, she was treated as a contender—only to be dropped when the movement collapsed in 1935. With the exception of a partly Jewish female fencer, the German team had no Jewish participants.

The American Team

That still left open the racial composition of the American team, which did include a number of Jews. As it happens, the 1936 Olympics are remembered in large measure for the superb performance of America's black athletes, especially the sprinter Jesse Owens, who took home four gold medals. Certainly Hitler was repelled by the presence of blacks on the victory podium—he had privately expressed the wish that they be banned from the competition altogether—but this was one aspect he was unable to control.

The Soviets treated with contempt the [International Olympic Committee's] cherished concept that sport should be independent of politics.

Nevertheless, the Nazi dictator could only have been delighted by the results on the playing fields, where German athletes racked up 33 gold medals, nine more than the second-place United States. With fascist Italy finishing third, and Britain and France lagging dismally behind, Hitler was not the only observer to conclude that the 1936 Olympics certified the decline of the democracies and the coming ascendancy of the Reich. Nor could he have been dissatisfied with the IOC's complicity in the outcome.

The 1980 Moscow Olympics

If the award of the 1936 Olympics to Germany was tragedy, the IOC's decision to give the 1980 Olympics to the USSR was farce—of a particularly grisly kind. In 1974, when the decision was taken, Moscow was the nerve center of a global empire of cruelty that encompassed not only the vast territory of the Soviet Union but also the countries of Eastern Europe and a growing handful of outposts in the developing world. As recently as 1968, when the Red Army invaded Czechoslovakia, the Kremlin had made it clear that efforts to achieve a measure of freedom in its sphere of influence would be crushed by force. Though the mass arrests and executions of Stalin's terror had long since abated, dissident writers, intellectuals, and human-rights campaigners were still routinely being packed off to the Gulag [Soviet forced labor camps].

In designating Moscow as the Olympic host, the IOC was thus repeating its error of the 1930's. It was also impugning its own athletic principles. Like their totalitarian brethren in Nazi Germany, the Soviets treated with contempt the IOC's cherished concept that sport should be independent of politics. To the Soviets, such independence was an ideological absurdity. They had long recognized the propaganda value of athletic prowess, and the Olympics represented just another skirmish in the international class struggle.

Soviet Athletes

Like all other institutions in Communist society, organized athletics in the USSR were thoroughly controlled by the ruling Communist party. Over a period of decades, the State Committee on Physical Culture and Sport had established a powerful, officially financed juggernaut whose overarching purpose was to prove Soviet athletic superiority to the world. Accumulating gold medals in Olympic competition was one of its major points of focus. Since the Soviet model was duly copied by other Communist countries, international sports had evolved into two very different systems: a Western one that carefully preserved an athlete's status as an amateur and a Communist one in which athletes, amateurs in name only, were trained and treated as professionals.

China seems to have grasped from the outset of the selection process that its political system would not be an issue of overriding importance or stand as an insuperable obstacle to its Olympic plans.

Given the stakes as they saw them, it was no accident that the Soviets became notorious for flouting the basic rules of sport. At a moment when other countries were establishing testing regimens for performance-enhancing drugs like steroids, Moscow moved in the opposite direction, employing its state-run athletic and medical infrastructure to develop ever more powerful substances and ever more refined methods for eluding their detection. IOC officials, well aware of the practice, closed their eyes to it, as they did to the Soviet penchant for rigging results in other ways. In preceding Olympics and in a long string of other international competitions, the bias of judges from the Soviet Union and allied Communist states had become an open secret.

The Moscow Olympic Boycott

Only an accident of timing prevented the Kremlin's success in securing the 1980 Olympics from being capped by an undiluted propaganda triumph. Toward the end of 1979, Communist rule in neighboring Afghanistan had begun to unravel, and in December the USSR marched in to rescue the situation. American passivity in the decade of detente, especially in evidence under Jimmy Carter, had led Moscow to conclude it could act with impunity. But a stunned Carter responded to the invasion with a package of sanctions whose most important item was a boycott of the forthcoming Moscow games.

Carter's boycott decision was met with a hailstorm of opposition, both by some in the U.S. who saw it as too weak and by many others who saw it as too strong. The IOC rejected out of hand a proposal to find an alternative venue for the games; echoing the pieties of his predecessors in the 1930's, the IOC president, Lord Killanin, grandly declared that "the Olympics should not be used for poitical purposes." Carter even found it difficult to persuade the U.S. Olympic Committee to adhere voluntarily to his policy; at one point, he was compelled to threaten legal sanctions if American athletes chose to defy him.

The boycott faced even greater opposition from America's allies abroad. In particular, the refusal of Europe to participate in it led many observers to conclude that Carter's initiative had failed. Indeed it had, in its own terms: the USSR did not withdraw from Afghanistan, and the games went on just as they had in Berlin in 1936. But now there was a difference: China, the USSR's bitter adversary, joined with the United States in staying away, and so did most of the Muslim world out of solidarity with the Islamic victims of Soviet aggression in Afghanistan. In the end, the absence of some 40 to 50 countries, not to mention of American television networks, delivered a bruising blow to Soviet morale.

The IOC was far more preoccupied with Beijing's environmental deficiencies than with its repressive politics.

True, the USSR collected a huge number of gold medals. But if the Kremlin had hoped to present a global audience with the image of a confident, efficient, and forward-looking superpower, the Moscow games became linked instead to the invasion of a small and defenseless country. This time around, the IOC would seem to have been taught a clear and painful lesson about the cost of placing its faith in a dictatorship.

China

Evidently not, however. Although Jacques Rogge, the current chairman of the IOC, has at least tacitly acknowledged that [2008's] host country is a closed society, he has predicted confidently that the games will "open up China." He also seems to be hoping that the People's Republic cannot meaningfully be compared with Nazi Germany or Soviet Russia.

About this he is right—up to a point. China today has peaceful relations with its neighbors (Taiwan partially excepted), boasts one of the world's most dynamic economies, and is a far freer place than it was in the heyday of Chairman Mao. A new and more politically aware middle class is emerging. To many observers, progress toward greater freedom is all but inevitable. The Olympics themselves, as the [George W.] Bush administration contended in supporting Beijing's bid, could prove a "powerful but intangible incentive" for democratic change.

It is estimated that over a million residents have been forcibly evicted, with an undetermined percentage of them left homeless.

Unfortunately, China seems to have grasped from the outset of the selection process that its political system would not be an issue of overriding importance or stand as an insuperable obstacle to its Olympic plans. It had reason to think this. In 1993, a mere four years after the massacre in Tiananmen Square [where Chinese military fired on and killed protesters], China was only narrowly defeated in its attempt to gain the 2000 games.

During the run-up to the IOC decision in that earlier instance, the Chinese had maneuvered to soften their image by releasing several high-profile political prisoners. This time they did not bother. To the contrary: at the very moment when the IOC was entering its final deliberations, Beijing stepped up its persecution of both the Falun Gong religious sect and independent journalists.

Environmental Deficiencies Versus Repressive Politics

As the Chinese may have foreseen, the IOC was far more preoccupied with Beijing's environmental deficiencies than with its repressive politics. There were fears that the heavy cloud of soot and smog that perpetually hangs over the capital city would weaken performance on the field and irritate spectators. And here was an issue on which the Chinese were prepared to respond with alacrity.

As part of its formal bid, Beijing laid out an elaborate "action plan" to create "a new image of Beijing." This grand scheme centered on a drastic improvement in air quality, sweeping changes in the character of the city's neighborhoods, and major upgrades in its transportation system. Specific steps for accomplishing these goals were carefully spelled out. Some 200 high-pollution factories would be relocated to sites outside the city; "green zones" would be established throughout Beijing; the sand storms that regularly blow in during the summer would be reduced through a massive project to reverse soil erosion in surrounding regions; the subway system would be expanded to cut automobile exhaust fumes and traffic congestion; clean natural gas would replace dirty coal as the city's primary heating fuel.

We have already had some inkling as to how these undertakings are to be met—and at what human cost. In February 2001, during a visit to Beijing by an IOC inspection team, the Chinese authorities placed an ad-hoc moratorium on the use of coal to heat apartment buildings, producing a temporary improvement in air quality and no doubt impressing the IOC with China's ability to act decisively—while also leaving millions of residents without heat in the dead of winter.

In dealing with the media, the authorities prefer to rely on a sophisticated regime of regulations designed to encourage self-censorship.

This was but a prelude to more far-reaching and permanent measures to modernize Beijing, including especially the massive destruction of older housing. Already it is estimated that over a millon residents have been forcibly evicted, with an undetermined percentage of them left homeless. Those subject to "relocation"—primarily the poor and migrant workers from the provinces—enjoy no right of appeal or protest concerning the level of compensation set by the state, and those who do object risk imprisonment. The displacement has taken place in an information vacuum, with virtually no coverage by the controlled domestic media and very little by the international press.

Censorship

Like much else in post-Mao China, media censorship has been modernized to suit the needs of a country now extensively involved with the outside world. Editors of Chinese newspapers have been instructed to stress the social benefits that will accompany the Olympics, and to avoid anything that might raise questions about the price being paid by the Chinese people. This is the same system that has successfully suppressed news about the defective merchandise produced in China for both domestic and foreign consumption and the spread of contagious agricultural and human diseases like SARS.

In dealing with the media, the authorities prefer to rely on a sophisticated regime of regulations designed to encourage self-censorship. But, when necessary, they are also prepared to use an iron fist. Today's China leads the world in the number of imprisoned journalists and the number of individuals charged with criminal offenses for "misusing" the Internet. Nor is it shy about intimidating foreign newsmen or native Chinese working for foreign outlets. Shortly after the IOC voted to approve Beijing's bid, the authorities arrested Zhao Yah, an employee of the *New York Times*'s Beijing bureau, on charges of violating state secrets. The charges, later reduced to fraud, appeared to be baseless, and after serving a full three-year sentence, he was released.

It is the most sinister and shocking features of a dictatorship that are the likeliest to emerge when it hosts the Olympics.

Controlling Protests

A major focus of Chinese concern has been the possibility of spontaneous or organized street demonstrations during the games themselves. Protests of this kind occurred prior to the Seoul games of 1988 and are widely regarded as having played a pivotal role in bringing about the collapse of South Korea's military dictatorship. The Chinese are determined to avoid even a hint of the Korean experience. In their Olympic action plan, they promised "tight but friendly and peaceful security measures"; since then, as a preemptive measure, they have instituted policies that are neither friendly nor peaceful. In line with the clear predilection of the regime for avoiding unseemly publicity, officials have increasingly made use of house arrests and detention without trial as a means of silencing dissidents who might otherwise be emboldened to air their grievances to the foreign press. At the same time, lengthy prison terms for expressing "subversive" views are far from uncommon.

The Chinese have also been developing a strategy to deflect or control potential protests by foreigners. China's intelligence services have launched an extensive information-gathering operation to pinpoint foreign organizations that might cause trouble during the games. "Trouble," of course, means peaceful picketing, demonstrations, marches, press conferences, and the like—the sorts of actions that are perfectly legal in democratic settings. The IOC, for its part, has already indicated where its sympathies lie; an official has described plans for citizen protests at the Olympics as "regrettable."

A Complicated Society

How will things play out? It is hard to know in advance. Some members of Congress, spurred on by Chinese dissidents, have begun calling for a Western boycott even as President Bush has accepted an invitation to attend. Wherever such foreign factors might or might not lead, there is no escaping the fact that today's China is an exceptionally complicated society with subterranean currents that we can hardly discern. The Chinese authorities themselves might well be in the dark about what the Olympics finally portend and, as their recent clampdown suggests, may indeed have begun to fear adverse repercussions. In August [2007], American newspapers were full of stories about a swine virus, the blue-ear pig disease, that had spread to 25 of China's 33 provinces, killing off a large fraction of one of the country's most important herds. Characteristically, the government kept its own public and the rest of the world officially unapprised of the nature and extent of the disease, leaving it to private journalists and foreign sources to ferret out what they could.

If the past is any guide, it is the most sinister and shocking features of a dictatorship that are the likeliest to emerge when it hosts the Olympics. For Germany in 1936, it was anti-Semitism and militarism; for the Soviet Union in 1980, it was imperial aggression. Whatever happens in China in 2008, there is no evidence that democracy will be enhanced, human rights will be improved, or the suffering of the Chinese people will be alleviated. As for the International Olympic Committee, it seems to have learned little or nothing from its own past mistakes. In fact, with the news of the IOC's decision to award the 2014 winter games to Putin's Russia, it seems bent on repeating them.

11

The Olympics Should Not Allow Performance-Enhancing Drugs

Runner's World

Runner's World *is an international magazine that provides news, information, and advice for runners, from running equipment reviews to training techniques to races and marathons.*

In the following viewpoint, the editors of Runner's World *discusses the problem of performance-enhancing drugs in the sporting industry, specifically in running. They talk with Frank Shorter, the national spokesperson for the United States Anti-Doping Agency (USADA), which is responsible for drug testing of Olympic sports in the United States, and a few other experts about their opinions on performance-enhancing drugs. All of the panelists agree that doping constitutes cheating and undermines the sport because it enables athletes to falsely improve their race times. The participants talk about the ongoing use of performance-enhancing drugs in professional sports and the Olympics in spite of the severe consequences, and discuss ways of solving the problem.*

O n July 29 [2006], news broke that Justin Gatlin, co-owner of the world record for the 100 meters, tested positive for testosterone after an April meet in Kansas. Word of Gatlin's failed test—coming just three days after reports that Tour de France winner Floyd Landis also had tested positive for test-

Runner's World, "The Straight Dope," September 9, 2006. www.runnersworld.com. Reproduced by permission.

osterone—left runners and sports fans alike shocked, angry, and feeling a bit duped. Gatlin had gained a following for his recent success on the track (gold in the 100 meters at the 2004 Olympics, victories in the 100 and 200 meters at the 2005 World Championships), as well as his antidrug position off it. He was a powerful voice, especially among young runners, for achieving success naturally, not synthetically. Gatlin now faces banishment from the sport, and his coach, Trevor Graham—long linked to runners tainted by doping charges—has been barred from U.S. Olympic Committee training facilities.

In light of the Gatlin revelations, *Runner's World* assembled a panel of track and distance-running leaders, via teleconference, on August 3 [2006] to discuss the sport's seemingly perpetual drug problem and how it can be solved once and for all. Our experts: Frank Shorter, national spokesperson for the United States Anti-Doping Agency (USADA), which is responsible for drug testing of Olympic sports in this country; Craig Masback, CEO of USA Track & Field (USATF); Mary Wittenberg, race director of the ING New York City Marathon; and U.S. Olympic marathoners Deena Kastor and Alan Culpepper. (Representatives for Gatlin declined requests to make the runner available to us.) The five shared their frustrations and varying solutions—including calls for federal-government intervention and jail time for athletes caught doping—and debated the virtues of drug-testing procedures even while Culpepper was undergoing a random drug test at his home in Colorado. . . .

Runner's World: *How did you react to the Gatlin news? Does his positive test indicate a prevalent drug problem in our sport?*

Frank Shorter: I was not surprised. Having been connected with USADA, I get enough information about what's going on not to be surprised. And as far as how prevalent the problem is, I don't think that matters anymore. The point is, it's a huge problem when the people at the absolute top of your sport are involved. It's not really a matter of how many people are doing it; it's having a system that works to deter as many people as you can.

There are a few who are cheating, and we just need to make sure that the rules are so strict and so enforced that it's not worth getting caught.

Deena Kastor: I was actually shocked. Justin has been such a great role model and spokesperson for USA Track & Field, talking with children about avoiding drugs and getting to the top on your own accord. I think for every clean athlete, this is their worst nightmare. Now, anyone who speaks about [drug use] has this lack of credibility to their words.

Mary Wittenberg: The moment I found out my reaction was, our sport is at a significant risk here. And that this is a moment to take very seriously and to do all we can to ensure we don't get back here.

RW: *There seems to be a pervasive belief that most people at the elite level, and those who win races or break records, are dirty.*

Kastor: I don't believe that most athletes are dirty. There are a few who are cheating, and we just need to make sure that the rules are so strict and so enforced that it's not worth getting caught. At both Olympic Games I've been to, surveys were passed around with questions like, "If you can earn a gold medal but die in five years, would you do it?" And more than 50 percent of the athletes said yes. We need to make sure that desire isn't so great.

Craig Masback: Both my personal experience as an athlete, which was largely in a pretesting era, and my experience in this job tell me that the vast majority of athletes are doing it the right way. Having said that, I was profoundly disillusioned by this development. [Gatlin] was an athlete who by all appearances understood not only what was important about winning the correct way but also what his responsibility was with respect to speaking about that to others. . . .

RW: *Alan, when you go to the start of a major championship race—the World Championships, the Olympics—and you look to the left and to the right, do you wonder who's clean and who's not?*

Alan Culpepper: Well, first off, in an ironic twist, I'm in the process of being drug tested by USADA as we speak.

RW: *What exactly does that mean?*

Culpepper: We're in the waiting phase. Richard [the test sample collector] is waiting for me to get hydrated since I just finished a long run. But to answer your question, on the starting line [who's not clean] is not something I'm consciously thinking of. It's more in analyzing people's performances and the way they do it and the way you can see it in their faces. Over the years I've become more accustomed to picking up on the people I suspect, and I definitely think it's prevalent in the sport.

RW: *What's in people's faces that makes you suspicious?*

Culpepper: In watching European track meets, I don't know what it is, but you can tell that [some athletes'] performances are unnatural. You can see it in their agony, you can see it in their split times. And some of their finishing times just seem unnatural.

Shorter: I understand completely what Alan in saying. They just don't get tired in the same way. I had that feeling at the 20-mile point in the 1976 Olympic Marathon going through the University of Montreal. Something happened during the race and you go, This isn't right. I think there's something very important that goes beyond the question of how many people do you think are [doping]; it's the percentage advantage if you do it. Very simply, in a marathon for men, the advantage is four minutes; for women, it's five or six minutes. Use that as you judge whether or not you think certain people in a race would have the incentive. [The drug] EPO is worth two percent.

I improved 10 seconds in the mile in two years. In this day and age, rather than that being appreciated and respected, I would be suspected.

Culpepper: Going back to the facial expression. I feel like their coaches and their agents should be whispering to them, "It's supposed to hurt a little more than that." They almost accidently run too well. I know how I feel with a lap to go— even when I'm having the best performance of my career. I know how much struggle it takes to make a great performance—and some people look like they're just waiting till the last lap to run an all-out quarter. There's no fatigue factor....

Masback: The magic of our sport is the ability for someone to have a breakthrough. I improved 10 seconds in the mile in two years. In this day and age, rather than that being appreciated and respected, I would be suspected. I would never want Deena taking her time down to 2:15 or Alan going down to 2:06 and being in a similar position. And that is what is at stake here if we can't get it right.

RW: *Then what's got to be done to prevent this from continuing?*

Masback: This can't be something that can be solved only by sports organizations and anti-doping authorities. The government has to get involved, on two levels: 1) to make it criminal and punitive; and 2) to add the funds to make the testing better. Those two levels, combined with one other: the lifetime ban or significant ban for EPO or steroid use. It used to be a four-year ban, and European countries, over the objections of the United States, lobbied for a two-year ban. Last summer we proposed the lifetime ban to the IAAF [International Association of Athletics Federations], which rejected it but did agree to argue before WADA [the World Anti-Doping Agency] at its upcoming meeting next winter to move the two-year ban to four years. It would be better if it were lifetime, but at least there's talk within the communities of increasing the penalty. Furthermore, the testers have to be given a fuller range of options for catching people so we can continue to fight the battle. . . .

RW: *Why is progress so slow? Frank, you know what it's like to lose something to a drug cheat. But decades later we're still talking about doping and about two of the highest profile athletes in sports. It feels like nothing has changed.*

Shorter: Well, it has changed because the USOC decided in 2000 to create USADA. You have to see all that has been done in six years. Since 2000, the EPO test has come on line and the human growth hormone test will soon be here.

We have to get extreme, and it has to be criminal, and it has to be monetary.

Wittenberg: I think there's progress, too. Several people getting caught has shown that. If you go back to the 2004 Olympics and the Greek sprinters [Kostas Kenteris and Katerina Thanou, who were later charged by the IAAF with doping violations] and now Landis and Gatlin, it is certainly sending the message, "You're getting caught." I think that while this is a bottom-of-the-barrel moment, in terms of realizing how pervasive this may be, it is a moment to celebrate. I hope it will start to scare others who may be in similar situations. That fear didn't exist four years ago. . . .

RW: *Deena and Alan, are you encouraged or discouraged that people are getting caught?*

Culpepper: I'm encouraged when the biggest names in our sport and others are being caught. That is a big step forward. I still feel we're just scratching the surface. There's more that needs to be done, and deterrents have to be greater. We have to get extreme, and it has to be criminal, it has to be monetary. Regina Jacobs would be a convicted criminal, and to me that has to be the deterrent. [Jacobs, the former world and American 1500-meter indoor record holder, was suspended in 2004 for testing positive for the banned steroid THG.] If you are going to spend time in jail, that is a deterrent moving forward. To me, it has to be something people can grasp onto— not like, "You will be a shame to your family and you will regret this the rest of your life." We've had that forever, and it hasn't been a deterrent. It has to be a penalty that's greater than the incentive to cheat.

Kastor: We need to have criminal sentences and scratch past results and try to get prize money back.

12

The Rules Against Performance-Enhancing Drugs Are Arbitrary

William Saletan

William Saletan is national correspondent for Slate *magazine.*

Athletes do all kinds of things to their bodies to prepare them for competing in sports, including training in high altitudes, eating red meat and a lot of carbohydrates, and using performance-enhancing drugs. Despite the fact that several federal and medical organizations have vouched for the safety of these drugs, the World Anti-Doping Agency has banned their use. Furthermore, WADA has banned the use of other substances, even if they are not drugs, are not harmful to the body, and are not artificial. The list of prohibited substances changes constantly without notice and differs from sport to sport, and even between the sexes. As such, the rules governing performance-enhancing drugs make no sense.

On the first day of the [2006] Winter Olympics, Japanese ski jumper Masahiko Harada was disqualified before he could get out of the gate. The official reason was that his skis were too long for his weight. The real reason was that he had lost too much weight for his skis. Seven ounces too much, to be exact. That's the life of an Olympic athlete. Your most crucial piece of equipment, the one you hone for four years, is your body. It has to be perfect. If possible, better than perfect.

Every athlete knows how to exceed perfection. A steroid here, a hormone there, and you've got the speed, power, or stamina to get the gold. The International Olympic Committee knows it, too; hence the 1,200 drug tests being conducted at the [2006] Turin Games. Thanks to pharmacological data on the Internet and a blossoming generation of chemical hackers, athletes are finding new ways every day to alter their bodies for advantage. It's a multiplying mess of techniques and designer drugs, with varying degrees of risk, artificiality, and manipulation. And the dope cops have done a lousy job of sorting it out.

The World Anti-Doping Code

The bible of Olympic drug testing is the World Anti-Doping Code, written and enforced by the World Anti-Doping Agency. The code bans a substance or procedure if it meets any two of these criteria: 1) it endangers the athlete's health; 2) it "enhances sport performance"; or 3) it "violates the spirit of sport." Things that pose clear health risks—very high hemoglobin levels, for instance—are easy calls. But what about things that don't? If all enhancements were forbidden, the code points out, we'd have to ban training, red meat, and carbohydrate loading. That would be preposterous. But in the next breath, the code says enhancement through gene transfer "should be prohibited as contrary to the spirit of sport even if it is not harmful."

How, exactly, does the spirit of sport forbid gene transfer but not carbo-loading? The code doesn't say. It defines the spirit of sport as "ethics," "fair play," "character," and a bunch of other words that clarify nothing. In fact, the definition includes "courage" and "dedication." Doesn't it take more courage and dedication to alter your genes than to snarf a potato? Human-growth hormone appears on WADA's "Prohibited List" of substances and methods, even though the Food and Drug Administration, the National Institutes of Health, and the

American Association of Clinical Endocrinologists have vouched, to varying degrees, for its safety. Evidently growth hormone violates the spirit of sport, but stuffing yourself with steaks doesn't.

The "Prohibited List"

That's just the beginning of the confusion. The "Prohibited List" tolerates performance-enhancing substances in your body if they're "endogenous" rather than "exogenous." Endogenous, according to the *Merriam-Webster Medical Dictionary*, means "caused by factors within the body." Exogenous means "not synthesized within the organism." That seems clear enough: You can use what's yours, not what's artificial. But four pages later, the list bans the use of "autologous" blood, which means blood "derived from the same individual." You can use what's yours, except when you can't.

What counts as artificial? Training at high altitude boosts your red-blood-cell count; the code says it would be absurd to ban this practice just because it enhances performance. Yet the IOC bars athletes in Turin's Olympic Village from using hypobaric tents, which simulate high-altitude air, and WADA is debating whether to ban them worldwide. Athletes from flat countries say they need the tents to match the conditioning of athletes from mountainous countries. You'd think that WADA chairman Richard Pound, who vows on his Web page to "level the playing field," would appreciate that rationale. If Mohammed can't go to the mountain, why shouldn't the mountain come to Mohammed? Instead, Pound rejects the tents as "artificial" and "tacky." He neglects to explain how putting thin air indoors makes it artificial.

Manipulation is another ill-defined target of doping regulators. The Prohibited List says you mustn't build up hemoglobin or other helpful substances through "chemical and physical manipulation." But if your hemoglobin count gets too high, you're allowed, even expected, to knock it back down through chemical and physical manipulation. Athletes who busted the hemoglobin limit on their first drug test in Turin have been interviewed while guzzling water to lower their counts for the next test. If water doesn't do the job, doctors point out, you can always bleed yourself; the rules don't seem to preclude it. Between tests, Canadian skier Sean Crooks of Canada corrected his hemoglobin level by relocating from the ski-training venue in the Alps to the Olympic Village, where he could get low-altitude air. Good thing he didn't do it in a tent. That would have been cheating.

Subject to Change Without Notice

The IOC's doping rules for Turin say that WADA's Prohibited List is "final and shall not be subject to challenge" by athletes. But every year, with little or no explanation, the list changes. Adrenaline and intravenous injections are prohibited; caffeine is now OK. American sledder Zach Lund was bounced from Turin for failing to notice that Line 3 of Section 5 on Page 3 of last year's changes to the Prohibited List—"Alpha-reductase inhibitors (finasteride, dutasteride) have been added as masking agents"—made the baldness pills he'd taken and disclosed for six years suddenly verboten. Even the selective applications change. Last year, substances previously banned "in men only" became illegal for both sexes, while two hormones previously banned in both sexes became illegal only for men.

The list, which also applies to leagues outside the Olympics, differs nonsensically from sport to sport. In billiards, you're allowed two-tenths of a gram of alcohol per liter of blood. In power-boating, you're allowed three-tenths. At a quarter of a gram per liter, you're sober enough to operate a flying death machine but not a cue stick. Often, the limits change for no stated reason. Last year, keeping your alcohol level below a tenth of a gram per liter would get you into skiing but not motorcycling. This year, you can get into motorcycling with the same alcohol level, and you can ski plastered.

I understand the doping cops' predicament. Performance enhancement is mutating so fast, they're just trying to ban what they can and make sense of the rules later. But as we've seen in figure skating and other aesthetic competitions, judges' irrational decisions can discredit the entire Olympics. Maybe that's the nature of art. Science should do better.

13

Some Performance-Enhancing Drugs Should Be Legalized

Bengt Kayser, Alexandre Mauron, and Andy Miah

Bengt Kayser is professor of exercise physiology at the University of Geneva, Switzerland. Alexandre Mauron is professor of bioethics at the University of Geneva. Andy Miah is a lecturer in media, bioethics, and cyberculture at the University of Paisley, Scotland.

While there is a definite need for rules in sport, prohibiting athletes from using performance-enhancing drugs is misguided. It does not make sense to ban the use of the drugs due to health issues because playing sports is inherently risky and dangerous. Instead, performance-enhancing drugs should be legalized and used under a doctor's supervision. There is little risk that permitting the use of these drugs would result in an increase in the rates of death and chronic illnesses among athletes. Furthermore, the costs associated with prohibiting the use of performance-enhancing drugs are escalating and the results are questionable.

The rules of sport define a level playing field on which athletes compete. Antidoping policies exist, in theory, to encourage fair play. However, we believe they are unfounded, dangerous, and excessively costly.

The need for rules in sports cannot be dismissed. But the anchoring of today's antidoping regulations in the notion of fair play is misguided, since other factors that affect performance—e.g., biological and environmental factors—are unchecked. Getting help from one's genes—by being blessed with a performance-enhancing genetic predisposition—is acceptable. Use of drugs is not. Yet both types of advantage are undeserved. Prevailing sports ethics is unconcerned with this contradiction.

We believe that . . . use of drugs should be permitted under medical supervision.

Another ethical foundation for antidoping concerns the athlete's health. Antidoping control is judged necessary to prevent damage from doping. However, sport is dangerous even if no drugs are taken—playing soccer comes with high risks for knee and ankle problems, for instance, and boxing can lead to brain damage. To comprehensively assess any increase in risk afforded by the use of drugs or technology, every performance-enhancing method needs to be studied. Such work cannot be done while use of performance-enhancing drugs is illegal. We believe that rather than drive doping underground, use of drugs should be permitted under medical supervision.

Legalisation of the use of drugs in sport might even have some advantages. The boundary between the therapeutic and ergogenic—i.e., performance-enhancing—use of drugs is blurred at present and poses difficult questions for the controlling bodies of antidoping practice and for sports doctors. The antidoping rules often lead to complicated and costly administrative and medical follow-up to ascertain whether drugs taken by athletes are legitimate therapeutic agents or illicit.

If doping was allowed, would there be an increase in the rate of death and chronic illness among athletes? Would athletes have a shorter lifespan than the general population? Would there be more examples like the widespread use of performance-enhancing drugs in the former East German republic? We do not think so. Only a small proportion of the population engages in elite sports. Furthermore, legalisation of doping, we believe, would encourage more sensible, informed use of drugs in amateur sport, leading to an overall decline in the rate of health problems associated with doping. Finally, by allowing medically supervised doping, the drugs used could be assessed for a clearer view of what is dangerous and what is not.

The role of the doctor is to preserve their patients' best interests with respect to present and future health. A sports doctor has to fulfil this role while maintaining the athlete's performance at as high a level as possible. As such, as long as the first condition is met, any intervention proven safe, pharmacological or otherwise, should be justified, irrespective of whether or not it is ergogenic. A doctor who tries to enhance the performance of their athlete should not be punished for the use of pharmacological aids, but should be held accountable for any ill effects. Rather than speculate on antidoping test procedures, resources should be invested into protecting the integrity of doctors who make such judgments.

Acknowledging the importance of rules in sports, which might include the prohibition of doping, is, in itself, not problematic. However, a problem arises when the application of these rules is beset with diminishing returns: escalating costs and questionable effectiveness. The ethical foundation of prohibiting the use of ergogenic substances in sports is weak. As the cost of antidoping control rises year on year, ethical objections are raised that are, in our view, weightier than the ethical arguments advanced for antidoping. In the competition between increasingly sophisticated doping—e.g., gene transfer—and antidoping technology, there will never be a clear winner. Consequently, such a futile but expensive strategy is difficult to defend.

14

There Should Be a Minimum Age for Some Olympic Sports

Nancy Rust

Nancy Rust is a former competitive gymnast and gymnastics coach in Seattle.

The minimum age for participation in international competition in gymnastics was raised from 15 to 16 in 1997, and some would like to raise it to 18. Raising the minimum age would encourage athletes to compete longer; many female gymnasts have stopped competing by the time they reach age 18. An older minimum age would also protect the health, confidence, and safety of younger gymnasts because they would have more time to learn and develop their skills. Young athletes would still be able to compete, just not at World Championships or the Olympics.

Bruno Grandi, president of the international gymnastics governing body (FIG), has been quoted as saying that he would like to raise the minimum age limit once again for international competition. In 1997, the age limit was raised from 15 to 16. Grandi has said in the past that he thinks the age limit should be 18 and just recently announced that he believes there should be *no* international competitions for juniors whatsoever.

There are many things to consider with regard to age limit but by and large, I am tempted to agree with Grandi—though not entirely.

Nancy Rust, "My Take on the New Age Limit," *perfect 10*, December 7, 2007. http://perfect10.rustyparts.com. Reproduced by permission.

Reasons to Raise the Minimum Age

Here are a few of my thoughts on the subject...

- Making the age limit higher will encourage athletes to stay in the sport longer. Athletes, especially on the women's side, will see that it's not necessary to stop the sport at 18. Gymnasts like Oxana Chusovitina, Svetlana Khorkina, Mohini Bhardwaj, and Annia Hatch have made it abundantly clear and I believe the FIG should encourage that.... I believe that the rise of the event specialist will also encourage longevity in the sport.

- Raising the minimum age will further foster proper progression and technique for young athletes because there is plenty of time to develop. This is essential for physical safety, mental confidence, and assurance in execution.

- Allowing more time before being eligible to compete on the senior level would perhaps be easier on the athletes, both physically and mentally. Not only would slower progression be better on young women's bodies but Grandi is right to encourage mental maturity as well.

Valid Points Against a Minimum Age

There are many that disagree with Grandi and some have raised valid points. As Nadia Comaneci, who was 14 when she shot to international fame at the 1976 Montreal Olympics, pointed out, ... banning junior athletes from all international competition "will put gymnasts from small and developing countries at a disadvantage."

"Countries like the U.S. are so big, and have so many good gymnasts, that the state of Oklahoma could compete against Nebraska and it would be strong competition," she said. "But what about the small countries with like, 10 gymnasts total. Who will they compete with?"

I agree with Nadia. I don't think international competitions like the Junior Pan Ams should be discontinued. There is no reason that younger athletes shouldn't get a chance to compete with other countries. But the World Championships and Olympic events should be reserved for senior athletes.

15

A Minimum Age for Some Olympic Sports Is Unfair

Sharron Davies

Sharron Davies made her Olympic debut at age 13 in Montreal in 1976, swimming for Britain in the 200- and 400-meter individual medleys. She won a silver medal in the 400-meter individual medley at the 1980 Olympics in Moscow.

Imposing a minimum age requirement for some Olympic sports is unfair to the young athletes. Participating in the Olympics gives young athletes added experience that they will need when they are older and competing. Young athletes need to learn how to deal with the pressure and the long hours of training their sport requires. Many young athletes are not novices at competing at the international level; they have competed against the same athletes in other competitions. Moreover, the demands and maneuvers required in some sports are best performed by athletes who are younger and more agile than older competitors.

To a certain extent it depends on the individual as to whether they are ready for an Olympics, and [British diver Tom Daley] is a very mature young man. If you have heard him in interviews, he is very aware, very astute and very bright: all the things he needs to be to compete at this level.

Invaluable Experience

Beijing [2008] will give him an Olympics under his belt and that experience will be invaluable when it comes to London 2012 where he is hoping to win a gold medal. That is exactly

Sharron Davies, "Debate: Is 14 Too Young to Compete at an Olympic Games? No," *Guardian* (UK), February 27, 2008. Reproduced by permission of Guardian News Service, LTD.

what Montreal did for me in 1976. When it came to Moscow four years later I wasn't overawed by the experience of being at an Olympics. I knew what to expect and I knew I was there to do a job.

It was only at the age of 29 in Barcelona 1992 that I was able to really make the most of the Olympic experience and enjoy every moment because I felt so lucky to have had another chance to make the team. When I won my medal the situation was clouded by politics, while in Montreal I wasn't old enough to fully appreciate everything. It will be a similar situation for Tom in Beijing.

The age is relative to the sport.

It is the Olympic Games. When you have trained for six hours a day, year after year, there is a lot of pressure that comes from the desire to win. What he has to learn is how to deal with that so that he can perform on one day and win a medal. Being in Beijing can only benefit him to that end. And remember that he is not a novice at international level. Tom has been competing against the same divers who will be at the Olympics for the past 18 months.

People have to understand that a lot of divers are very young. The age is relative to the sport. This is not a situation where we are talking about a 14-year-old sprinter being picked for the 100m. It would not be physically possible for them to compete. But Tom's shape and size are absolutely perfect. The Chinese divers who will be his main competitors will all be of a similar age and build.

Tom also has very protective and supportive parents, while the British Olympic Association is very aware of the pitfalls that can await young competitors and has policies in place to make sure they are kept safe.

It is very difficult to compare sports and the age limits they enforce. One of the reasons gymnastics took the decision to raise the age of Olympic competition to 16 was because of the allegations of drugs being forced on gymnasts to keep them small and the lack of restraint on how far young children would be driven. It was also an attempt to get back to a situation where elegance rather than flicks and tumbles was at the centre of the sport. But you cannot use the same argument in diving where acrobatics are so significant.

Along comes Japan's Mao Asada, who turned 15 too late—a measly 87 days too late—to make the 2006 Olympics. But the ISU still allowed her to travel the world and compete in all the other major competitions this year (so much for school and normalcy). In the process, Asada became a media darling, winning the Grand Prix final, the biggest event of the year prior to the Olympics, by landing six triples, including the difficult triple axel, in her long program.

But the Games will go on without her, which means the ISU has created a situation in which a figurative asterisk will most assuredly be placed by the name of whoever wins the women's gold.

And what of Asada? If you're thinking there's always the next Olympics, consider that the way skating works, she could very well be too old by 2010.

16

Transgendered Athletes Should Be Allowed to Compete

Alison Carlson

Alison Carlson is a former sports coach and founding member of the International Association of Athletics Federations' International Work Group on Gender Verification.

Gender verification in Olympic sports is a gross violation of privacy. While several female athletes have been confirmed or rumored to be male, many of the women who were tested were born with aberrant chromosomes, lived as women, and had no idea of their uncertain sex. Male-to-female transsexual athletes have little physical advantage over women athletes who were born female. Hormone therapy and the removal of male organs result in loss of muscle bulk and strength, and a reduction of speed. Few male athletes will go through years of hormone therapy and surgery on a whim just to compete—and possibly win—as a woman. The decision by the International Olympic Committee to allow transsexuals to compete as women is progressive and fair.

The entire concept was appalling, an invasion of privacy. We had no problem with men. Maybe some of the women were born with abnormalities, but I had no problem, if they were born that way and lived as women in the rest of their lives. I hated what they did to them. It wasn't called for. It wasn't their fault. Drugs were and are the real problem. I

Alison Carlson, "Suspect Sex: Effects of Gender Verification Tests Used on Olympic Athletes," *Lancet*, v. 366, no. 9503, December 17, 2005, pp. S39–40. Copyright © 2005 The Lancet Publishing Group, a division of Elsevier Science Ltd. Reproduced by permission.

couldn't understand what factors they thought they could use to determine womanhood for sports anyway. Just look at my birth certificate. —Track legend Wilma Rudolph, 1989

Precedent for gender verification in women's sports was set at the 1936 Berlin Olympics, when Polish journalists accused American gold medalist Helen Stephens of being a man. Officials felt compelled to do a sex check and issue confirmation that Stephens was indeed female. The 6-foot-tall Stephens, said to have long male-like strides, had beaten Polish-American track legend Stella Walsh in the 100 m. Ironically, when Walsh was shot in the crossfire of a store robbery in 1980, the coroner's report, leaked to the press, indicated ambiguous genitalia and abnormal sex chromosomes.

Other instances cited as justification for the International Olympic Committee's mandating of so-called femininity control in 1968 involved four world-class athletes who lived and competed as women, but who later through surgery became men—Czech runner Zdenka Koubkova, who held a world record in the 800 m in 1934; Lea Caurla and Claire Bressolles, French track medallists at the 1946 European Cup; and Austrian ski champion Erika Schinegger, who retired after a 1967 medical examination requested by World Cup authorities revealed irregularities. Schinegger underwent sex reassignment and then competed in men's skiing and cycling. Both Schinegger and Bressolles were reported to have married and fathered children. There was only one documented case of a man actually masquerading as a woman. In the mid-1950s, Hermann (also known as Dora) Ratjen from Germany announced that he had been persuaded by Nazi officials to pose as female in the 1930s. He qualified for the women's high jump finals at the Berlin Olympics—where he finished fourth—and then set a world record in 1938.

Not long after Ratjen's announcement, rumours circulated that men from one Eastern Bloc country [countries in Eastern and Central Europe who were allies of or controlled by the

Soviet Union] were binding their genitals and passing themselves off as women in competition. As a consequence, the femininity of several dominant Eastern Bloc competitors in the 1950s and 1960s was questioned. Most notable because of their strength and appearance were the famous Press sisters, Tamara and Irina. The greatest Soviet track and field athletes of that era, they set 26 world records and won six Olympic gold medals between them. At the 1966 European Cup athletics championships, however, when women were asked for the first time to undress in front of a panel of gynaecologists, neither the Press sisters nor four others whose sex was suspect showed up. Their absence was construed as confirmation that they were not really women. In reality, they were most likely one or another form of intersex assigned by doctors to the female gender (or simply assumed to be female) at birth, trying to do the best they could in life as women and athletes.

Genetic screens were, simply, discriminatory, since women born with aberrant chromosomes have no unfair, male-like physical advantages.

Thus in 1967, with close-up visual examination of the external genitalia added to screening protocol (and follow-up chromosome analysis done especially in this case), Polish sprinter Ewa Klobukowska unfortunately became the first woman banned from sports for failing the sex test. Though neither hypermuscular nor notably more successful than her peers, and even though she had passed the so-called nude parade a year earlier, officials told the 21-year-old she had been competing unwittingly as a man because she had male-like irregularities and, accounts suggest, XX/XXY mosaicism. Klobukowska was publicly disqualified, and recognition of her 100 m world record and Olympic medals was removed from the books. She became severely depressed and broke off all contact with the sports world.

Athletes had mixed reactions to the policy of blanket chromosome screening when it was introduced. Most reflexively supported the policy as an effort to prevent unfair competition, and as a preferable alternative to nude parades. Others, however, knew—or gleaned over time—that this policy, meant to prevent men and male-like advantage in women's events, was singling out and harming women born with (and often unaware of) biological sex differentiation differences that confer no unfair advantage. Maria Patino, for example, understood the injustice intimately. After her diagnosis of complete androgen insensitivity and an XY chromosome complement was leaked to the press, Patino's sports career as a hurdler seemed over; she was thrown off the national team and out of the athletes' residence. People pointed at her on the street, friends disappeared. She went into hiding, trying to cope with the knowledge that she would never have children. "If I hadn't been an athlete, my femininity would never have been questioned," she said. "What happened to me was like being raped. It must be the same sense of violation and shame. Only in my case, the whole world watched. . . ." Rather than give up, though, she enlisted help from specialists in sports and medicine to build an appeal for reconsideration, and in 1988 became the first person to be requalified as a woman for sport. Patino never recovered her form, but her case did galvanise serious, informed opposition to genetic screening of sportsgirls and sportswomen.

If the results of individuals whose sex was difficult to ascertain had been proven to be unattainable by genetically typical women, the rationale behind sex chromosome screening might have had more merit. But the records of known and suspected athletes of uncertain sex have consistently been superseded by XX women who passed sex tests, and their results never approached those of male counterparts. Genetic screens were, simply, discriminatory, since women born with aberrant chromosomes have no unfair, male-like physical advantages that XX women who pass tests cannot have as a matter of other forms of biological variation.

Hormone therapy and removal of male organs result in considerable diminution of speed, muscle bulk, and strength.

A history of post-pubertal male-to-female transsexuals in sports (normally developed men surgically reassigned) has contributed to paranoia about unfair male-like physical advantage. In 1975, at age 41 years, Richard Raskin became Renee Richards and won a battle in US courts for the right to compete in women's professional tennis. Over 5 years, she won one small title and got to the finals of the US Open doubles. In 1987, 50-year-old Charlotte Wood, nee Charles Wolff, garnered wary public attention and open hostility when she competed in two amateur US Golf Association events.

Richards and Wood ignited unfounded concern that floodgates would open to other, possibly younger, transathletes. As one transathlete noted, though: "No one goes through years of hormone therapy, massive surgery and this permanent life change on a whim, just to compete." Furthermore, automatic assumptions about advantage are medically discounted: hormone therapy and removal of male organs result in considerable diminution of speed, muscle bulk, and strength. Taller-than-average height and some potential biomechanical advantages might remain, but doctors point out that transathletes who carry a male skeletal structure on a female-type musculature are more prone to injury.

These realities are probably why the current transathletes Mianne Bagger, an Australian professional golfer, and Michelle Dumaresq, Canadian professional downhill mountain biker, have received warmer receptions than Richards and Wood did. Aged 28 years when she underwent surgery, Bagger has been welcomed as a professional by Ladies Golf Australia, and now plays Ladies European Tour events. At 1.78 m, 68 kg, she drives the ball 219.5 m, and is petitioning the Ladies Professional Golf Association for acceptance. Dumaresq was 26 years old when she transitioned in 1996. She started competitive downhill racing 5 years later. Reviewing her case after rivals complained, the international mountain bike governing body affirmed her eligibility, and Dumaresq is now Canada's national champion.

Increased awareness over time of the ethical and functional inconsistencies of reducing women athletes to their sex chromosomes explains the decision by the International Olympic Committee in 1999 to eliminate blanket chromosome screens; and in 2004 to proactively establish a progressive policy to allow transgender competitors in Olympic games provided they are at least 2 years post surgery and on continued hormone therapy. Any attempt to separate the sexes for sport by use of black and white constructs of maleness/femaleness creates more problems than it solves. Chromosome screens imposed these cut and dried distinctions, which simply do not exist biologically.

That society has had a difficult time allowing for sex/gender identity difference is affirmed by the ending to Stella Walsh's story. Walsh was raised a girl, and was a much-loved athlete, wife, and coach. Nevertheless, after she was killed in 1980, there was uproar about her gender in the media, and Walsh is still referred to in some record books as a he/she.

17

Transgendered Athletes Have an Unfair Advantage

Barbara Amiel

Barbara Amiel is a right-wing columnist who has written for the London newspaper Daily Telegraph *and the Canadian magazine* Maclean's.

An English bill that allows people to change their gender simply by making a declaration—or living as the other sex for two years—hovers close to the line of senselessness. Many men have superior hand-eye coordination over women, as well as advantages in speed and strength. If transsexuals are allowed to compete under their new gender, they should have to do so with a handicap. Transsexuals who compete have an unfair desire to win against handicapped competition.

Most people in the world know if they are male or female. A junior filing clerk called Vicky was my first encounter with a different response. Back then, in the early 1960s, James Morris, the travel writer, had not yet become Jan Morris, author of *Conundrum*, the compelling story of Morris's sex change. For Vicky, we were still in the Dark Ages.

She was at once both the happiest and unhappiest person. The masculine stubble on her face was unconvincingly covered with Max Factor pancake make-up. Next to sex-change surgery, her single most desired goal was to be able to use the ladies' loo. A minute's conversation with Vicky, for which she was extravagantly happy, was enough to show any sentient

Barbara Amiel, "Women May Have It Better, But Not Everyone Wants to Be One," *Telegraph* (UK), January 3, 2004. Reproduced by permission.

person that, for its sufferers, gender confusion is a nightmare of [Dutch painter] Hieronymus Bosch proportions.

England's Gender Recognition Bill

But that was then and this is now. Today [January 3, 2004], Parliament gives a second reading to the Gender Recognition Bill. As a liberal or libertarian, one wants people to be able to do whatever they want, so long as they don't harm others.

A sex-change operation may do wonders for their gender identity and sex life, but it doesn't eliminate the superior hand-to-eye co-ordination with which men seem blessed, nor all their advantages in speed and strength.

Consequently, it's difficult to be upset by a Bill that simply recognises that we all exist on a sliding scale between such things as health and sickness or normality and freakishness. Being healthy is not meritorious in itself. Being freakish is not a character flaw. We are as nature intended. And any decent society ought to mitigate whatever bad things flow from its variations.

But at a certain point you cross the threshold that separates senselessness from common sense. At a minimum, aspects of the Gender Recognition Bill hover close to the line. The tipover may be this: to permit any person who is clearly both in their physical attributes and their chromosomes one of the two existing genders, to switch genders simply by means of a declaration accompanied by a sympathetic or politically inclined specialist's attestation.

If gender is only a matter for some gender recognition panel's decision, I can't see how we can prevent the next obvious step: people declaring themselves another gender and sending a postcard to the authorities kindly requesting their new birth certificates.

Transsexuals and the Olympics

In our muddle, we are turning reality on its head. The Gender Identification Bill has an opt-out clause regarding athletes to allow the International Olympic Committee to decide—in the name of EU [European Union] equality—whether to allow transsexuals to compete under their new gender identity. The proposal would allow them to compete in their acquired gender not only after sex-change surgery but also before it, if they have lived as a woman for two years.

In the bad old days of the Soviet Union, it was impossible to tell who was what. One could only collapse in fits of laughter at the "female" East German swimming team. The only known example of gender cheating was an admission in 1955 by a German athlete that he had pretended to be a woman in the 1936 Olympics. But all that was comprehensible. Communist and Nazi societies were intrinsically immoral: they cultivated he-women athletes to get medals for propaganda purposes.

Unless transsexuals are prepared to compete under their new genders with a handicap . . . what is before the IOC is . . . an unfair desire to win against handicapped competition.

Today's transsexual athletes have no such excuses. A sex-change operation may do wonders for their gender identity and sex life, but it doesn't eliminate the superior hand-to-eye co-ordination with which men seem blessed, nor all their advantages in speed and strength. Our passion for "equality" has not yet banned male and female categories in sport because, in most areas, with the possible exception of synchronised swimming, men have a natural superiority.

An Unfair Advantage

Unless transsexuals are prepared to compete under their new genders with a handicap—perhaps two games per set in tennis or 30 metres in the 100 metre sprint—what is before the IOC is not a question of gender identity, but rather an unfair desire to win against handicapped competition. This is not a gender issue, but a moral one. Which may be why the IOC doesn't seem to have any petitions from women wanting to compete as men.

Confused Identity

But if you can't beat them fairly, join them. The *Daily Mail* featured a stunning woman named Samantha Kane in a décolleté evening dress. Next to her photo was one of a handsome, moustached young man of Iraqi origin, named Sam Hashimi. Below was a photo of Charles Kane, a face of almost feral beauty and head of longish blonde hair. Turns out all three are the same person. Sam had a sex-change operation and became Samantha, but after a few years wanted to be Sam again, so he is midway into it as Charles.

The *Mail* in its inimitable way, had ferreted out one of several patients complaining that a London psychiatrist specialising in gender identity disorder had switched them over too fast. Sam, or rather Charles, claimed that he had observed that his wife had an easy life—lunching with girlfriends while he slaved over a hot telephone brokering deals. When the wife left him, getting a good financial settlement and custody of the children, his envy of the female of the species grew even greater and he fantasised about being a woman. In this depressed state, he was referred to a GID specialist, who, rather swiftly, cut off Sam's unhappiness. But then, inter alia, the glamorous Samantha got bored with female sex and shopping and realised that she had been prematurely operated upon. Now the General Medical Council is investigating.

Living in this particular corner of hell is nothing to joke about. Still, this is a man bites dog story, a freakish manifestation of human sexuality. Sam-Charles's insight into the way society dishes out more spoils these days to women is perfectly valid. However, it's a thought that almost every man going through a divorce may have, as well as quite a few who are not. A gender-secure male whose wife leaves him does not fantasise about dressing up in women's clothing; he does not have a sex-change operation, no matter how persuasive his therapist. If the recognition that women have it better were all it takes to want gender re-assignment surgery, there would be mile-long queues around Harley Street.

Psychological gender seems to be a sliding scale and most of us are comfortably at the top end, while transsexuals suffer at the bottom. But some poor lost souls are marooned somewhere in the middle. Heaven knows how any consultant or Gender Identification Board can do the right thing for them.

In writing about the sovereignty of Parliament, [British journalist Walter] Bagehot remarked that "Parliament can make and unmake every law, . . . interfere with the course of justice, extinguish the most sacred private rights of the citizen . . . but even Parliament cannot make a man a woman." Never mind the citizens' private rights, Bagehot could not possibly have imagined how Parliament would one day extinguish our private parts. Even Caligula [Roman ruler known for his cruelty] might have been impressed.

The Olympics Should Allow a Disabled Athlete to Compete

David Meller

David Meller is the editor of the blog The Sight is in End.

Oscar Pistorius, a runner from South Africa who was born without bones in his lower legs and so runs on prosthetic "legs," does not have an advantage over able-bodied runners. It takes Pistorius longer to get up to speed on his prosthetics than able-bodied runners. Even though his spring-like legs give him incredible speed, Pistorius has not run fast enough to beat the times of the best able-bodied runners. It is highly unlikely that any runner will amputate his legs in order to run on the prosthetic legs Pistorius uses.

The decision to ban 400m paralympian Oscar Pistorius—or "Blade Runner"—from running in the Beijing Olympics (were he to run the required qualifying time of 45.55 sec—the 'A' standard that South Africa will probably abide by) is an indictment on the IAAF [International Association of Athletics Federation] and world athletics.

In an age where drugs still damn the sport, . . . the IAAF has missed an opportunity to not only close the gap further between able-bodied and disabled athletes, but to restore interest, pride and above all, the central element of what makes athletics so memorable: the breaking down of mental and physical barriers.

David Meller, "Pistorius decision is wrong," *The Sight is in End*, January 14, 2008. http://thesightisinend.wordpress.com/2008/01/14/pistorius-decision-is-wrong. Reproduced by permission.

Prosthetic Legs Are Not an Advantage

Of course, Professor Peter Bruggemann [director of the Institute of Biomechanics and Orthopaedics at the German Sport University] believes that Pistorius could attain an advantage over able-bodied athletes with his use of prosthetic limbs, meaning the breaking down of these so-called barriers could be easier. However, with a personal best of 46.34—good enough to win gold at the 1932 Olympics—Pistorius isn't going to do that just yet.

I'll never understand how someone with no lower limbs could attain an advantage. I'll also never understand how the IAAF is taking the findings of one group of scientists as fact, rather than seeking opinions from a variety of scientists.

Pistorius' 'legs' are believed to take up to 30 meters to become effective, and as anyone who has ever watched a modicum of athletics before, it is the start that wins or loses races at smaller distances.

I cannot believe that Pistorius' 'cheetahs,' an ironic name in this instance, can match technique, hard work and the capacity of the human body. I also cannot believe that the acceptance of Pistorius will lead to a sort of *carte blanche*, where much improved artificial limbs arrive and usurp able-bodied athletes, or worse (and this has been mooted), where athletes have amputations in favour of enhanced characteristics.

It seems deeply offensive to Pistorius to even raise those issues on the back of his emergence. This is not someone who had his limbs amputated out of choice; this is someone who wants to be recognised as an able-bodied athlete, and on the same playing field—or in this instance, on the same running track.

The thought of anyone committing 'techno-doping' is in the realm of [science fiction author] Philip K. Dick, and would never be allowed, nor would it occur. Talking illegal substances is one thing, having an amputation and a subsequent fitting of a new, false limb is quite another.

A Sentimental Sporting Event

There is also the argument that sentiment should not have a place within sport. But the Olympics is, and always has been, the most sentimental of sporting events, so why end here? Its very being is sentimental. And in an Olympics that could well be remembered more for pollution, postponed events and China's human rights record, the story of one man could have helped light up an Olympics that could well be in danger of major embarrassment.

You also have to question whether the IOC would agree with having an athlete with false limbs competing with perceived specimens of athletic brilliance. It seems absurd when in past years you've had wild-card entrants, whilst adding to the Olympic spirit, preventing more competent athletes from competing.

And yes, Pistorius' participation in the Olympics could have an effect on the Paralympics which is getting successively bigger and more successful. But what more does he have to achieve at that level? Could there be a point where his dominance in the Paralympics could have a negative effect? Or will he become the Games' primary selling point? Couldn't that be just as negative? With someone like Pistorius, is Dame Tanni Gray Thompson's view that the Paralympics is a "parallel games" relevant?

It is such a complete debate, and I could have gone on for thousands of words. But in 1954, Roger Bannister broke the four-minute mile—that most recognisable of athletic barriers, which encompassed the mental frailties of breaking something thought impossible, and push the human body to its limit.

In 2008, we could have Oscar Pistorius breaking down an additional barrier. He has an appeal pending at the Court of Arbitration for Sport in Lausanne [Switzerland], and we could have had the purest achievement in athletics for many years— and I mean pure in the most literal of meanings.

The Disabled Athlete Has an Unfair Advantage

Amby Burfoot

Amby Burfoot is editor-at-large for Runner's World *magazine and the winner of the 1968 Boston Marathon.*

The prosthetic running "legs" of Oscar Pistorius, a double-amputee sprinter, give him an unfair advantage against able-bodied runners. His legs are actually springs, and the manufacturers of prosthetic legs are developing better—and faster—legs every day. Pistorius does not need to train harder in order to qualify for the Beijing Olympics, he just needs a better set of equipment. The prosthetic legs work differently than human legs, and as such, give him an unfair advantage. He should not be allowed to compete against able-bodied runners.

I know I'd be smart to ignore the bait and leave this subject alone, but I just can't resist. [In June 2007], the IAAF [International Association of Athletics Federations] apparently told South Africa double-amputee sprinter Oscar Pistorius that he's free to compete in international competitions this year, including the World Championships. What have these people been smokin'?

Let me say this in my defense: I have a sister who's an amputee. I support all reasonable rules and regulations for challenged athletes. The IAAF has adopted a cautious and prudent

Amby Burfoot, "Oscar Pistorius, the Sprinter with the Artificial Legs, Doesn't Belong in the Olympics," *Footloose: Amby Burfoot's Notes from the Road*, June 24, 2007. http://footloose.runnersworld.com/2007/06/i-know-id-be-sm.html. Reproduced by permission of Rodale, Inc.

approach, saying it wants to encourage more research before making any doors-slammed-in-your-face decisions. . . .

Track Legs Versus "Social" Legs

[There's a photo that] shows Pistorius walking onto a track for a workout. He's wearing his track legs while carrying another pair of legs, his "social legs" we might call them. The clear implication: The track legs are faster than the social legs. Today. And there's nothing to stop them from becoming even faster tomorrow. And the day after that. The manufacturers of prosthetic legs aren't exactly resting on their laurels. They're developing better legs every day. Hate to bring this up, but the war in Iraq is a powerful stimulus, given all the injured, and the Army's funding of medical research for them.

The IAAF doesn't have an end-of-the-world-as-we-know-it situation on its hands. Not yet anyway. Pistorius's best time in the 400 meters, 46.56, isn't good enough to qualify him for the Beijing Olympic Games, where the "A" and "B" standards are 45.55 and 45.95. So far this year, which hasn't yet entered the big European season, 20 athletes worldwide have run 45.26 or faster. To be a second behind world-class runners, as Pistorius is, amounts to a huge gap.

A Better Set of Equipment

But the gap is the point. Pistorius doesn't have to narrow it by training harder. He only needs a better set of equipment.

A mechanical leg and a human leg are vastly different equipment.

In 1975 Bob Hall became the first athlete to complete the Boston Marathon in a wheelchair, clocking a 2:58. In 1980, Curt Brinkman wheeled the course in 1:55:00. Three years ago [2004] Ernst Van Dyk rolled Boston in 1:18:27. That's an improvement, in 30 years, of roughly 100 minutes. Mostly because of better, faster equipment. During the same period, the men's course record has dropped less than 3 minutes to Robert Cheruiyot's 2:07:14. Because human physiology is notoriously difficult to enhance. Without drugs. Or better equipment. . . .

A mechanical leg and a human leg are vastly different equipment. The latter has an unmatched "intelligence," which is why you can run on both dry concrete and soft sand. A mechanical leg is dumb; it has to be chiseled and "tuned" to its task; it can't run on both concrete and sand. If Pistorius were to run both the 100 meters and 10,000 meters, he would probably chose different prostheses for each, since the biomechanical forces are different between the two.

The rest of us don't get to make choices like this. We're forced to sprint, run marathons, and do triathlons with the same set of legs (amputee triathletes often use different legs for bicycling and running.)

Pistorius is an inspiration, as are all challenged athletes who strive to be the best they can be in their given fields. I hope he keeps running track, and also that he rises to the top in business, politics, the arts, or whatever his chosen field might be. I'm glad that the Olympic movement includes a Paralympic Games, where athletes like Pistorius can win gold medals and set world records, as he already has. I feel fortunate every day to have been born ably-bodied, and wouldn't exchange places with Pistorius for anything.

But I don't believe he belongs in the World Championships or Olympics. He's running on hardware, not normal legs and feet. And when the sport is running as opposed to, say, Scrabble, chess or archery, your legs and feet make all the difference.

Organizations to Contact

The editors have compiled the following list of organizations concerned with the issues debated in this book. The descriptions are derived from materials provided by the organizations. All have publications or information available for interested readers. The list was compiled on the date of publication of the present volume; the information provided here may change. Be aware that many organizations take several weeks or longer to respond to inquiries, so allow as much time as possible.

Canadian Center for Ethics in Sports
350-955 Green Valley Circle, Ottawa, Ontario   K2C 3V4
   Canada
(613) 521-3340 • fax: (613) 521-3134
e-mail: info@cces.ca
Web site: www.cces.ca

CCES promotes drug-free sports in Canada and in international competition. Among its responsibilities is the administration of drug tests in Canadian athletic programs. Information available on the Web site includes educational materials, annual reports, and research papers, such as *The Sport We Want Final Report* and *Ethical Challenges and Responsibilities Regarding Supplements*.

Dream for Darfur
c/o Public Interest Projects, 80 Broad Street, Suite 1600
New York, NY   10004
(646) 823-2412 • fax: (917) 438-4639
Web site: www.dreamfordarfur.org

Dream for Darfur is a coalition of advocacy groups, such as nongovernmental organizations, human rights groups, Olympic athletes, and organizations concerned about Tibet, that are trying to pressure the Chinese government to use its influence with the Sudanese government to end the genocide in Darfur, by using the 2008 Summer Olympics in Beijing as a lever. These groups and individuals believe that China is complicit in the genocide because its purchase of oil from Sudan buys the guns used in the genocide. Dream for Darfur does not support a boycott of the Olympics. Among the publications available on its Web site is the report *Foul Play: How the International Olympic Committee Failed the Olympic Charter and Darfur.*

Human Rights Watch
350 Fifth Avenue, 34th Floor, New York, NY   10118-3299
(212) 290-4700 • fax: (212) 736-1300
Web site: http://china.hrw.org

Human Rights Watch is dedicated to protecting the civil rights of people around the world. It monitors and investigates violations of basic human rights and generates public pressure to confront human rights abusers and convince them to change. Human Rights Watch believes that the 2008 Olympic Games in Beijing give the Chinese government a unique opportunity to demonstrate to its people and the world a commitment to the fundamental freedoms guaranteed in the Universal Declaration of Human Rights and in China's own constitution. Its publications include the annual *World Report* and the report *Media Freedom.*

International Association of Athletics Federations
17 rue Princesse Florestine   BP 359 MC98007
   Monaco
e-mail: info@iaaf.org
Web site: www.iaaf.org

The IAAF was founded in 1912 by 17 national athletic federations (membership is now more than 200) who saw the need for a governing authority, for an athletic program, and for standardized technical equipment and official world records. Its Web site contains information about antidoping, and its publications include the newsletter *IAAF News* and *IAAF Magazine.*

International Olympic Committee

Chateau de Vidy, Lausanne   CH-1007
  Switzerland
Web site: www.olympic.org

The IOC oversees the Olympic Games. It determines which cities will host the games and sets policies on drug use, and on transgendered and disabled athletes. Its antidoping code prohibits the use of steroids and other performance-enhancing drugs. The Web site provides information on the World Anti-Doping Agency, which was established under the initiative of the IOC, banned substances, and related matters.

International Paralympic Committee

Adenauerallee 212-214, Bonn   53113
  Germany
e-mail: info@paralympic.org
Web site: www.paralympic.org

The IPC is an umbrella organization that oversees athletes with all types of disabilities in several sports. It holds and oversees the Paralympic Games, an international sporting competition that is parallel to the Olympic Games. Its Web site provides information on antidoping and sport science.

National Center for Drug Free Sport

2537 Madison Avenue, Kansas City, MO   64108
(816) 474-8655 • fax: (816) 502-9287
e-mail: info@drugfreesport.com
Web site: www.drugfreesport.com

The National Center for Drug Free Sport manages most aspects of the National Collegiate Athletic Association's (NCAA) drug-testing program. Additional resources provided by the center include the Dietary Supplement Resource Exchange Center and a speakers bureau. The center publishes the quarterly magazine *Insight*, the current issue of which is available on its Web site. Also on its Web site are news articles about drug use in sports.

National Clearinghouse for Alcohol and Drug Information
PO Box 2345, Rockville, MD   20847-2345
(800) 729-6686 • fax: (240) 221-4292
Web site: www.health.org

The clearinghouse distributes publications of the U.S. Department of Health and Human Services, the National Institute on Drug Abuse, and other federal agencies concerned with drug abuse. Available brochures include *Tips for Teens About Steroids* and *Anabolic Steroids: A Threat to Body and Mind.*

United States Anti-Doping Agency
1330 Quail Lake Loop, Suite 260
Colorado Springs, CO   80906-4651
(866) 601-2632 • fax: (719) 785-2001
e-mail: webmaster@usantidoping.org
Web site: www.usantidoping.org

The USADA manages the drug testing of U.S. Olympic, Pan Am Games, and Paralympic athletes and enforces sanctions against athletes who take banned substances. The agency also teaches athletes about the risks and ethics of steroid abuse. USADA issues annual reports and the quarterly newsletter *Spirit of Sport.* Its Web site provides access to Drug Reference Online, a database of currently banned drugs. The Web site's *Cheating Your Health* link provides resources on the health risks of performance-enhancing drugs.

United States Olympic Committee
One Olympic Plaza, Colorado Springs, CO   80909
(719) 632-5551
Web site: www.usoc.org

The USOC is a nonprofit private organization that coordinates all Olympic-related activity in the United States. It works with the International Olympic Committee and other organizations to discourage the use of steroids and other drugs in sports. Information on USOC programs can be found on the Web site.

World Anti-Doping Agency
800 Place Victoria, Suite 1700, P.O. Box 120
Montreal, Quebec   H4Z 1B7
   Canada
(514) 904-9232 • fax: (514) 904-8650
e-mail: info@wada-ama.org
Web site: www.wada-ama.org

WADA is an independent international antidoping agency that works with governments, athletes, international sports federations, and national and international Olympic committees to coordinate a comprehensive drug-testing program. Its publications include annual reports and the magazine *Play True*, recent issues of which are available on its Web site. WADA's Web site also publishes a doping quiz, information on banned substances and drug-testing laboratories, and a searchable database.

Bibliography

Books

John Bale and Mette Krogh Christensen — *Post-Olympism? Questioning Sport in the Twenty-first Century.* New York: Berg, 2004.

Rob Beamish and Ian Ritchie — *Fastest, Highest, Strongest: A Critique of High-Performance Sport.* New York: Routledge, 2006.

Andrew Billings — *Olympic Media: Inside the Biggest Show on Television.* New York: Routledge, 2008.

Susan Brownell — *Beijing's Games: What the Olympics Mean to China.* Lanham, MD: Rowman and Littlefield, 2008.

Jeff Caraccioli and Tom Caraccioli — *Boycott: Stolen Dreams of the 1980 Moscow Olympic Games.* Washington, DC: New Chapter Press, 2008.

Paul Close — *The Beijing Olympiad: The Political Economy of a Sporting Mega-Event.* New York: Routledge, 2006.

Vassil Girginov and S.J. Parry — *The Olympic Games Explained: A Student Guide to the Evolution of the Modern Olympic Games.* New York: Routledge, 2005.

Caroline Hatton — *The Night Olympic Team: Fighting to Keep Drugs Out of the Games.* Honesdale, PA: Boyds Mills Press, 2008.

John M. Hoberman — *Testosterone Dreams: Rejuvenation, Aphrodisia, Doping.* Berkeley: University of California Press, 2005.

Grant Jarvie, Dong-Jhy Hwang, and Mel Brennan — *Sport Revolution and the Beijing Olympics.* New York: Berg, 2008.

Nathan Jendrick — *Dunks, Doubles, Doping: How Steroids Are Killing American Athletes.* New Guilford, CT: Lyons Press, 2006.

Charles F. Levinthal — *Drugs, Behavior, and Modern Society,* Boston, MA: Allyn and Bacon, 2005.

David Maraniss — *Rome 1960: The Olympics that Changed the World.* New York: Simon and Shuster, 2008.

Michael Payne — *Olympic Turnaround: How the Olympics Stepped Back from the Brink of Extinction to Become the World's Best-Known Brand.* Westport, CT: Praeger, 2006.

Dick Pound — *Inside the Olympics: A Behind-the-Scenes Look at the Politics, the Scandals, and the Glory of the Games.* Etobicoke, Ontario: Wiley, 2006.

Monroe E. Price and Daniel Dayan, eds. — *Owning the Olympics: Narratives of the New China.* Ann Arbor: University of Michigan, 2008.

Christopher A. Shaw — *Five Ring Circus: Myths and Realities of the Olympic Games.* Gabriola Island, British Columbia: New Society, 2008.

Kristine Toohey and A.J. Veal — *The Olympic Games: A Social Science Perspective.* Cambridge: MA: CABI, 2007.

David Wallechinsky and Jaime Loucky — *The Complete Book of the Olympics.* London: Arum Press, 2008.

Minky Worden — *China's Great Leap: The Beijing Games and Olympian Human Rights Challenges.* New York: Seven Stories Press, 2008.

Guoqi Xu — *Olympic Dreams: China and Sports 1895–2008.* Cambridge, MA: Harvard University Press, 2008.

Periodicals

Glenn Dickey — "Cheating: Just Part of the Game," *San Francisco Examiner*, February 16, 2007.

Economist — "For a Wreath, a Flag—or Cash?" August 14, 2004.

Ronan Farrow and Mia Farrow — "The 'Genocide Olympics,'" *Wall Street Journal*, March 28, 2007.

Norman Fost — "Let the Doping Begin," *Seed*, February 21, 2006.

Nancy Gibbs — "Cool Running," *Time*, January 28, 2008.

Nat Hentoff — "Boycott 2008 Genocidal China Olympics?" *Jewish World Review*, April 17, 2007.

Philip Hersh
"Age-Limit Rule Doesn't Add Up for U.S. Skating," *Los Angeles Times*, January 29, 2008.

Hu Jia
"The Real China and the Olympics," *Guardian*, February 27, 2008.

Kenneth Jost
"Sports and Drugs," *CQ Researcher*, July 23, 2004.

Phelim Kine
"Where's the IOC's Voice on Press Freedom in China?" *Globe and Mail*, November 8, 2007.

Dionne L. Koller
"Trampling Athletes' Due Process Rights," *Baltimore Sun*, March 29, 2007.

Nicholas D. Kristof
"China's Genocide Olympics," *New York Times*, January 24, 2008.

Joshua Kurlantzick
"Why the Olympics Are Bad for China," *New Republic*, February 27, 2008.

Jere Longman
"A Fair Race?" *New York Times Upfront*, October 1, 2007.

Arne Ljungqvist and Myron Genel
"Transsexual Athletes—When Is Competition Fair?" *Lancet*, December 17, 2005.

Normandy Madden
"Marketers Limber Up for 2008 Beijing Olympics," *Advertising Age*, October 30, 2006.

Mark Magnier
"China Feels Heat of Olympic Flame," *Los Angeles Times*, February 13, 2008.

Maria Jose   "A Woman Tried and Tested," *Lancet*,
Martinez-Patino   December 17, 2005.

Rona Marech   "Olympics' Transgender Quandary,"
                    SFGate.com, June 14, 2004.

Mark McClusky   "Nix the Ban on Sports Drugs,"
                    Wired, September 21, 2005.

Josh McHugh   "Blade Runner," *Wired*, March 2007.

Matthew J. Mitten   "Is Drug Testing of Athletes Neces-
                    sary?" *USA Today*, November 2005.

National Institute "Anabolic Steroid Abuse," *Research*
on Drug Abuse   *Report Series*, September 2006.

New York Times   "Empty Olympic Promises," February
                    4, 2008.

Timothy D.   "Tainted Glory: Doping and Athletic
Noakes   Performance," *New England Journal*
                    of Medicine, August 26, 2004.

Sophie   "Olympic Word Games," *Wall Street*
Richardson   *Journal*, August 8, 2007.

Linda Robertson   "Today's U.S. Olympians Have a
                    Wealth of Talent—and Funding,"
                    Miami Herald, February 18, 2006.

Joshua Robinson   "Olympic Dream Stays Alive," *New*
and Alan Schwarz   *York Times*, May 17, 2008.

Julian Savulescu,   "Why We Should Allow
Bennett Foddy,   Performance-Enhancing Drugs in
and Megan   Sport," *British Journal of Sports Medi-*
Clayton   *cine*, August 1, 2005.

George Vecsey   "Admirable Spirit, but Rules Are Rules," *New York Times*, January 10, 2008.

George Vecsey   "A Ruling on the Side of Opportunity," *New York Times*, May 20, 2008.

Jim Yardley   "Before Olympic Games, China Quells Dissent," *International Herald-Tribune*, January 29, 2008.

Index